Merry Christmas
Bobby, hope you
enjoy this as
much as I did
buying it for you.
Aunt Gladys

1965

MICKEY MANTLE: *Mister Yankee*

In this up-to-date portrait of the amazing Mickey Mantle, the power hitter of the New York Yankees, the author endeavors to acquaint readers with the "real" Mickey Mantle. Although the records he has achieved tell some of the story, there is still more. This is the life story of the great outfielder and most popular ballplayer in baseball today, the 1962 winner of the American League Most Valuable Player award.

MICKEY MANTLE

MISTER YANKEE

By Al Silverman

G. P. Putnam's Sons   New York

Second Impression

© 1963 by Al Silverman

All rights reserved

Published simultaneously in the Dominion of Canada
by Longmans Canada Limited, Toronto

Library of Congress Catalog Card Number: 63–13994

Manufactured in the United States of America

10-up

CONTENTS

For Tommy

A switch-hitter too,

and a believer

MICKEY MANTLE: MISTER YANKEE

CHAPTER ONE

BOOS NO MORE

The moment that changes a man's life. Rarely is it possible to put the finger on that moment and say, "This is when it happened."

When did it happen for Mickey Charles Mantle? When did the sullen crowd shed its sullenness, the reserved crowd shed its reservations? When did respect overwhelm disrespect, admiration replace resentment? When did the boos change to cheers and when was it that Mickey Charles Mantle left the doghouse and joined the shrine with the other super heroes—Babe Ruth, Lou Gehrig, Joe Di-Maggio?

When did the crowd forget, finally, that Mickey Charles Mantle was not another Joe DiMaggio, but his own man, his own unique man?

It happened not all at once, not in one grand moment, but in a progression of moments involving events and personalities—a bad ball game, a good ball game, a team-mate named Roger Maris, a manager named Casey Stengel, and one named Ralph Houk—and of course, the principal actor, Mickey Mantle himself.

All these moments can be charted. Looking back now, they fall into a grand design, as if arranged by a computer. But it was no grand design to Mickey Mantle, especially not that one moment nine years into his major league career—when he failed to run out a ground ball.

It was Sunday, August 14, 1960, Yankee Stadium in the Bronx, New York. The New York Yankees had been fight-ing all season to regain a pennant they had lost the year before. But the Chicago White Sox and Baltimore Orioles were fighting the Yankees step for step. And now the Yankees were about to play a crucial doubleheader with the Washington Senators.

When the public address announcer read off the Yankee starting lineup, there was the customary genial applause for the home players—Cletis Boyer, the lead-off man; Tony Kubek batting second; Yogi Berra batting third; Roger Maris batting fourth. But when the fifth batter was an-nounced, Mickey Mantle, the crowd of 29,970 reacted differently.

There were cheers, of course, the high-pitched hurrahs of young boys, who have always loved Mickey. But there were deep-throated adult boos, too, malicious in tone and strong enough to drown out the cheers.

Why the boos? Possibly because Mickey Mantle was not having a great year, batting only .273 at the time, though he had hit 27 home runs. Superficially, that could have been the reason, but there was more to it than that. Even in his super years of 1956 and 1957, when he won two Most Valuable Player awards, when he was everything that everyone had expected him to be—the boos could be heard.

Why? Because he was different from the man whose place he had taken in center field, Joe DiMaggio. Because he had none of DiMaggio's silent grace, and none of DiMaggio's disciplined temperament that enabled him to swallow the bad days with the good. When things went badly on the ball field for Mickey Mantle, he reacted in anger and in public. He was different from Joe DiMaggio, and that was one thing the fans found hard to reconcile.

Also, he was something short of the perfection that had been predicted for him. He had had those two great years, but why couldn't he win a triple crown every year? The fans had always demanded perfection of Mantle, had expected him to be the greatest ballplayer who ever lived. And when he fell short of that, the fans took out their frustrations on Mantle—forgetting that for all his great skills, he was, after all, just another human being like you and me.

And so when his name was announced on that hot August afternoon at Yankee Stadium, the boos were mighty and Mickey trotted out to his position in center field, head down, playing with his tangled thoughts brought on by the cold reception of the home audience.

In that first game, Mickey did nothing to extend his popularity. He got one hit in four at-bats. The Yankees dropped the opener to Washington, 5–4.

In the second game, Jack Kralick pitching for Washington against Eli Grba, it went better for Mickey for awhile—two singles in his first three appearances.

Then it came to the bottom of the sixth, the scored tied, 1–1, one out and Roger Maris on first base, Mantle moving up to the plate and Casey Stengel in the dugout, pawing back and forth; Mantle moving up to the plate, his bad right knee sore and tired as it has always been sore and tired in second games of doubleheaders.

Maris danced off first as young Kralick reared back and threw. Mickey swung, getting a thin piece of the ball and it skittered along the ground to third baseman Reno Bertoia. Bertoia fielded the ball cleanly and swept it on to second baseman Billy Gardner, who leaped over the high-sliding Roger Maris, firing the ball to first baseman Harmon Killebrew, rushing to make the double play.

But there was no need to rush. Mickey Mantle, tired and confused, had stopped running. He had made a mistake. He had thought there were two out.

Roger Maris was taken out of the game. He had painfully injured a couple of ribs, desperately trying to break up the double play.

Mickey Mantle was taken out of the game—for "loafing."

The Yankees lost it in fifteen innings and dropped to third place in the American League pennant race.

How many times have you seen major league ball-players commit mental boners? It is not uncommon. I saw one in the summer of 1962 when the Los Angeles Dodgers held a 12–0 lead over the New York Mets and Dodger catcher John Roseboro was tagged out after wandering off second base. He had thought there were two outs, not one. Dodger manager Walt Alston yanked him from the game, too, but there wasn't a line in the newspapers the next day about Roseboro's lapse.

But in the Yankee dressing room after a bitter double defeat, the reporters rushed to get the story on the Mantle banishment. First, Mickey himself was questioned.

"Was it your idea to come out?" one reporter asked Mantle.

"No."

"Was it Stengel's?"

"Must have been," Mickey said. "It wasn't mine."

In the manager's office, Stengel was assuring one and all that it had indeed been his idea.

"I took Mantle out," rasped the old man, "because he didn't run, and I'm tired of seeing him not run. If he is hurt and can't run, he should tell me."

Mickey Mantle could have slept better that Sunday night.

He awoke uncertainly. He read the papers and the headlines that blared about Casey Stengel's displeasure with his star ballplayer. And, later that afternoon, he went to Yankee Stadium uncertainly. But then the uncertainty vanished.

Mickey's Yankee teammates, practically to a man, came up to him and said that, heck, it wasn't so terrible making a mistake like that. They said, too, that the old man was dead wrong to have pulled him from the game. Mickey grinned that country boy grin of his and he felt better. And he felt, too, that there would be plenty of time to prove himself to Casey, and to his teammates.

The Baltimore Orioles, who were tied for first place with the White Sox, both a half game ahead of the Yankees, were coming in for the night game. And Mickey Mantle's name was in the starting lineup.

Running out to take his position in center field, Mickey was greeted by boos and whistles and handkerchief waving. And when in the first inning, Mantle hit Baltimore pitcher Jerry Walker's first pitch back to Jim Gentile at

first base for an easy out, the boos swelled and fell over
Mantle like hailstones. As Bobby Richardson trotted out
to hand Mickey his glove, a bleacher fan hollered, "Run it
out, Mickey." Grim-lipped, Mantle ran head down to
center field.

In the fourth inning, with the Orioles leading 2–0,
Hector Lopez singled. Mickey came up. Again, he heard
the boos. But he shrugged and waited. Pitcher Walker
leaned in and took the sign, Mantle watching intently.
The great neck muscles tensed, the great veined arms and
hands grew taut—and then Mickey uncoiled.

He uncoiled that rippling, thrilling swing of his. And
he connected. The ball rode high and far towards right
field. The Yankee relief pitchers in the bullpen turned
and watched the ball as it clattered against the rear fence
of the bullpen.

This time the crowd which had been sullen toward
Mantle two innings before could do nothing but applaud
the strength and beauty of that 400-foot home run that
tied the game for the Yankees. Mickey ran the bases
effortlessly, as he always does after he has smacked a ball
with satisfaction. He crossed the plate, his hand flicking
Bill Skowron's, the on-deck batter, and as he stepped into
the dugout, he flung his helmet aside and accepted the
backslaps of his teammates. Manager Stengel grunted ap-
preciatively.

But the game was not over and the applause that year of
1960 for Mickey Mantle was always fickle and unpre-
dictable, and a little rare. On his next at-bat, with Tony
Kubek on first base, Mickey hit a high fly ball to right field
to end the inning. This time the boos assumed command
again.

And so it went down to the last of the eighth. Baltimore

had scored a run in the top of the inning and now the
Orioles led, 3–2. Hector Lopez, first batter of the inning,
walked. Now Mantle came up to face the knuckle ball
relief artist of the Orioles, Hoyt Wilhelm.

The first pitch was a swinging strike, and immediately
the jackals started jeering. Mickey hit under the next pitch
and it rose high, but bleak behind the plate. Catcher Clint
Courtney dashed towards the screen. He stuck out the
oversized glove that he used to catch Wilhelm's knucklers.
The ball struck the edge of the glove, and bounced out.

That was all Mickey needed. With a two-strike count,
Mickey hit it and it was gone, gone into the right-field
seats.

This time the crowd stood up screaming as Mickey
rounded the bases, and this time Mickey responded. As he
crossed home plate, he tipped his cap to the fans and he
smiled.

The Yankees won that game and went back into first
place. Mickey had given them all their runs. In the dressing room afterward, he was a happy twenty-eight-year-old
man.

"I wanted to have a good game more than I've ever
wanted to have a good game in my whole life," Mickey
said. "When I came to the park, I was hoping for something nice to happen. I never thought it would turn out
as nice as it did."

It was Mickey's 29th home run of the year, and it
marked a turning point for the Yankees and for Mickey
Mantle. The Yankees were in first place again and Mickey
was hot. From that August 15th date to the end of the
season, Mickey hit another 11 home runs. The Yankees
beat off the challenge of the Orioles and then cooled off
the White Sox. His 40 home runs gave Mickey his third

Courtesy, *Sport* Magazine

Mantle at bat in the 1960 World Series against the Pittsburgh Pirates. Despite a key play by Mantle that helped to tie the seventh game in the ninth inning, the Pirates won the game and the series on Bill Mazeroski's home run in the bottom of the ninth.

American League home run title. His average was a below average for Mantle—.275—but he had driven in 94 runs and he had knocked the winning hit across in 20 Yankee games.

Those two days—one a day of humiliation, one a day of triumph—have to mark the turning point for Mickey Mantle in his relationship to his fans, and in his relationship to himself. But it didn't happen all at once.

It continued to build up after those two days. It built up during the 1960 World Series against the Pittsburgh Pirates, the Series the Yankees lost in the seventh game when Bill Mazeroski struck a clutch home run. In the third game of that Series, Mickey collected four hits. And when he trotted out to center field at Yankee Stadium in the fourth game, he was greeted by rapturous applause.

The fans also read that Mickey had cried in the clubhouse after the Mazeroski home run and this show of human emotion warmed them to him.

In 1961 the emerging Mickey Mantle image became clearer and clearer. The new manager, Ralph Houk, had designated Mantle as "leader" of the Yankees. But now there was the challenge of a teammate, Roger Maris. As Yankee sportscaster Phil Rizzuto put it, "I think the challenge of Maris inspired Mickey. He had been the number one man on the club until Maris came along and started clubbing those home runs. I think Mick rose to the challenge and this helped him a great deal."

This challenge from Roger Maris, a relative upstart, also drew the fans closer to Mickey. And when Maris toward the end of the '61 season overhauled Mantle in the home run race, and then smashed Babe Ruth's record of 60 home runs in one season, the boos for Mantle began to disappear completely.

It was a strange phenomenon that began in the first week of September and continued to the end of the season, when Mickey was struggling with an abscessed hip. And Mickey noticed it. When he hit his 52nd home run of the season against the Indians on September 1, the 42,000 fans at Yankee Stadium stood and cheered while he rounded the bases. Afterward, Mickey said, "I think it's because I'm the underdog now. People always go for the guy that's behind."

Whatever it was, it warmed Mickey Mantle. He told New York *Journal American* sports columnist Jimmy Cannon about his biggest thrill of the 1961 season.

"It was the game against Washington," Mickey said, "when I went into the game for defensive purposes in the ninth inning of the second game of the doubleheader. My arm was sore, I couldn't swing a bat. They really gave me a big hand. I never felt better in baseball. . . . I felt like I used to when I was playing high school football. You know, the band starts playing and they sing your school's song and you feel good."

That feeling persists today in the slowly approaching twilight of Mickey's baseball career. Today at Yankee Stadium, you hear an occasional bleat—"C'mon you sorehead, hit the ball!" But these are now the bleats of the minority. The boos, for the most part, are gone. Now the baseball public knows and accepts Mickey Mantle, with his limitations, for what he is. And what he is . . . well, it is very clear. He is a genuine super star who belongs alongside Lou Gehrig and Babe Ruth and Joe DiMaggio. And his place in baseball's Hall of Fame five years after he retires is just as certain as death and taxes and the hold that baseball in America has on all of us.

CHAPTER TWO

BUT WHO IS MICKEY MANTLE?

*H*e *is one of the elect now, one with DiMaggio, Ruth, Lou Gehrig and all the other old heroes.*

The words were written in the late fall of 1962 by the respected sports columnist Frank Graham. They were written just after Mickey Mantle was voted his third Most Valuable Player award. Only two other American League players, Joe DiMaggio and Yogi Berra, had ever won the "MVP," as it is called, three times. When Mickey Mantle heard that he had again won the most coveted honor in all of baseball, he said he was surprised and grateful—and that now he wanted to be the first player to win *four* MVP's.

This is Mickey Mantle today, the flame of desire burning as brightly as it did when Mickey was a teen-ager and learning about baseball from his dad.

But who is Mickey Mantle?

In appearance, Mickey Mantle looks like a physical marvel, and an all-American boy. He is a shade under six feet tall, a shade over 200 pounds in weight. He is a blond fair-faced man with a little boy's look, grey eyes and closely cropped brown hair, a crinkling boyish grin when things are going right, and a tight-lipped, slightly defiant scowl when things are going wrong.

And the body is like a weight lifter's body. The shoulders, arms and back are thickly muscled and he wears a size 17 collar. It is a body meant to scare pitchers. Once the old Indians pitcher Mike Garcia proclaimed, "When I'm working on Mantle, it looks like there's a great muscle running right down the middle of his neck. Pretty soon, that's all I can see. It's no fun for a pitcher to look at."

But who is Mickey Mantle?

The record tells some of it.

Through 1962, Mickey had played twelve major league seasons. In that time, he had led his league four times in home runs. He had hit a total of 404 home runs, putting him in the all-time elite "400 club." He had driven in 1,152 runs, again putting him up among the elite. He had scored 1,341 runs, leading his league in runs scored in six different years. He had a lifetime batting average of .309.

And of course he had been the core of the Yankee dynasty for those twelve years, years in which the Yankees won ten pennants and seven World Series.

But who is Mickey Mantle?

He is a family man, with a wife and four boys. He eats grapefruit juice, cereal, strawberries and milk for breakfast. He likes steaks for dinner, and also veal parmigan. He likes to watch Westerns on television and Westerns in the movies when he is on the road. He likes to read Westerns, but he also likes to read best sellers. He likes to listen to hillbilly music, but also to pop music. He likes to hunt quail and he likes to play golf. He likes life.

"My father died young," Mickey Mantle once said. "I'm not going to be cheated."

But who is Mickey Mantle?

He is a country boy who now spends most of his time in the big cities. He likes to dress casually, countrylike, but he is also a sophisticated big city dresser. He dislikes to speak in public but he is now an accomplished public speaker. He is a country boy who appreciates peace and silence, but he is also, to his teammates at least, one of the funniest men they know.

When Billy Martin, Mickey's old roommate, went into the Army, Martin received a big, brown manila envelope. Inside was a picture of Debbie Reynolds with an inscription. The inscription read: TO BILLY, THE MOST CHARMING MAN IN THE WORLD.

Mickey had written the inscription and sent the picture.

Another time in the summer of 1962 when Mickey was hobbling with a thigh injury, he came into the dugout from the dressing room with chewing tobacco pasted over one of his front teeth and his cap pulled down over his head, his ears sticking out. He walked the length of the dugout, talking and looking for all the world like the clownish Mortimer Snerd. He broke up the players.

In the spring of 1962 when he signed for the movie *Safe at Home*, with Roger Maris, Mickey looked into a mirror, put on a Marlon Brando stare and said, "I can't

A Yankee rookie in 1951, Mantle visits with some special fans in the grandstands. Merlyn Johnson is behind Mickey, his brother Ray peers over the shoulder of Mantle's father, who stands beside Mickey's mother.

understand how it could have taken them so long to dis-
cover me."

After the movie was filmed, a reporter asked Mickey if
he was glad it was over.

"Yeah," Mickey said. "And I told them my next movie
had to be a musical. No more roles as a ballplayer. I don't
want to be typed."

But who is Mickey Mantle?

He is a mortal and, like most mortals, full of contradic-
tions. Two of them:

One, his physical condition

Two, himself

He looks like Mr. America, but he has grievous physical
weaknesses. He has suffered from osteomyelitis in the left
leg since his high school days when he was kicked in a
football game. He threw out his right knee as a rookie in
the World Series of 1951 and it has never been the same
since. Today, even when he is healthy, he limps. He must
spend ten minutes before each game wrapping each knee
with yards of tight rubberized bandages.

Once Early Wynn, the crusty old White Sox pitcher
who hated batters, explained how much he respected
Mantle.

"I didn't like the way Mantle was bunting on me,"
Wynn said. "I figured he was taking advantage of my age.
I was going to rack him up. But I watched him bandage
his legs the last time I was in an All-Star game. I changed
my mind. I figured any guy with legs like that is hurting
himself more than me when he bunts."

Mickey once submitted to a locker room interview with
broadcaster Howard Cosell. The subject got around to
Mickey's legs.

Cosell said, "Mickey, as you sit there, I know that under

your stocking your right leg is taped from knee to thigh. Do you have to do that every day to play?"

Mickey said, "I think I could maybe do without it, but along about the fifth or sixth inning the leg would start to get tired. I tried to take it off in spring training, and I pulled the leg the first thing. If I let it off during the game, I would play all right and it would be easier to run without all the weight on it. But it would begin to ache toward the end of the game, so I wear it."

Cosell: "But still every game you play, along about the fifth or sixth inning, you're in pain along the right leg?"

Mantle: "It's according to the length of the game. If it's a fast game, say an hour and fifty minutes, the leg doesn't hurt nearly as much as if I had to stand out there for a four hour game."

Cosell: "Mickey, do you ever worry about the leg curtailing your career."

Mantle: "The only thing that worries me is that after a doubleheader, I come home and it hurts and you just got to worry about whether it's ever going to stop hurting or ever going to be as strong as it ever was again. That's the only thing I ever worry about. . . ."

He has pulled muscles in his legs and suffered other injuries traceable to the legs. "I can tell when I'm going to get hurt," he says. "I get tired and I start getting tight. Then I pull something. I can always feel it coming."

He blames his leg troubles on flat feet, but whatever it is, it has caused him to miss ball games. He has never had a year in which he has played in every single Yankee game. But he has also played in game after game in which he never should have. His teammates call him "B. and G." because of his courage—"blood and guts." This B & G was expressed best by Mantle himself one day when a writer asked him casually, "How do you feel?"

"Good," said Mickey. "Nothing hurts me except my legs. But they always hurt."

But who is Mickey Mantle?

The Mickey Mantle at war with himself.

Casey Stengel, who regarded Mickey as half a son and half a Stengel creation, was always exasperated by Mickey's temper tantrums. "The trouble with Mantle is Mantle," Stengel once said. "He'd always be great if he don't get mad at Mantle and fight Mantle when something goes wrong. Like one season in Boston when he bangs his fist against the dugout concrete after takin' a third strike. I hand him a bat and tell him to bang himself on top of the head with it, on account if he wants to end his career, he might as well do it quick and get it over with.

"Then when he gets mad at himself at bat, he goes to the field and they don't hit it over Mantle's head. They hit it over the other guy's head . . . the Mantle which Mantle's mad at. He stands out there in center field, his arms folded like this, giving this other Mantle heck and boom . . . suddenly somebody hits one and on account of the fight he's having out there, Mantle loses a step starting and the ball is gone and now he's madder than ever, and he keeps getting madder."

Mickey's teammates best understand these rages of Mantle. Says Whitey Ford, one of Mickey's best friends, "He wins ball games for us, so we don't mind what he does. The guys know he wins. They know he's the big hitter. They know he brings the fans into the park. Whatever he does helps everybody else and he does a helluva lot. If he gets a lot of dough, he's setting the standard. The rest of us will get more, too. Sure, I'm close to Mick, but I'm not just talking for myself. The other guys feel the same way I do."

"There are times," says another Yankee, "when he gets you sore because he's so darn sore at himself. You want to run up and tell him, 'Okay, you missed bad pitches twice. This is another time at bat.' But you don't stay sore because all of a sudden he busts one and you win a ball game."

Mickey Mantle is the first one to realize this side of Mantle. When, in the spring of 1961, Yankee manager Ralph Houk named Mickey as the "team leader," Mickey worried whether he could really be a leader with his temper. "How do you think it looks," he told writer Milton Gross, "for me to come back to the dugout after grounding out or something and take a kick at the water cooler? There are guys sitting in that dugout who maybe aren't playing or hitting .250 and they got to say to themselves, 'What's with that so and so?' Before I can lead anybody, I got to do something about myself."

"You mean," Gross asked, "that you're going to try and control your temper?"

"I've tried to control my temper," Mickey answered, "but I just don't think it's possible. I'm always going to get mad at myself for not doing good, but what I've got to do is not to do it in front of the others. If I've got to blow off steam, I've got to do it where nobody will see it."

But it is so difficult to change. Mickey fought himself as recently as the World Series of 1962, a Series in which he could only pick up three hits. Once, after striking out, he flung aside his batting helmet, then threw a punch at the concrete wall of the dugout. But he was also thirty-one years old and now had the grace to make fun of his problems.

In the locker room after Ralph Terry had whipped the Giants in the fifth game of that World Series, Terry put in a long-distance call to his wife in Oklahoma to tell her all about it. Mickey said, "When you're finished, call Merle [Mickey's wife] and tell her I went oh for four again."

Both Mickey and another super hero, Willie Mays, had a bad Series, and Mickey told a story of the guy in the bleachers at Yankee Stadium hollering at Mickey. "Hey, Mantle, everybody came out here to see who was better, you or Willie Mays. Now we wonder who's the worst."

An inning later, after Mickey had grounded out, the same voice hollered again. "Hey, Mantle. You win."

Mickey Mantle told that story on himself.

But who is Mickey Mantle?

The young Yankee players speak in awe when they speak of Mickey Mantle.

As Billy Martin once said, "For a man as big as Mickey is, he is exceptionally down to earth. There are a lot of guys who get a big head as soon as they get a big name. But not Mantle. There wasn't a rookie on our club who didn't feel free to come up and talk with Mickey."

In the spring of 1962 in St. Petersburg, Florida, the Yankees' training camp, Mickey once went up to a rookie, Lou Romanucci. He said, "Let's have a catch."

Romanucci was amazed. "Imagine," he said afterward, "me playing catch with Mickey Mantle."

Phil Linz, who was a utility infielder for the Yankees in 1962, remembers the day Mickey came to him. "He had seen my name on the list for tickets," Linz said, "and he asked me who I had coming. I told him my girl friend.

He said, 'Here, I got some box seats. You take them.' Boy, was my girl impressed."

Tom Tresh, American League rookie of the year in '62, was also overwhelmed by Mickey's attitude. When Tresh was shifted to left field from shortstop in midseason, he mentioned that he needed an outfielder's glove, somebody's old one maybe. "Mickey gave me a new one," Tresh told New York *Post* writer Leonard Shecter. "He gave me the new one he was breaking in for next year. I tried to give it back to him but he said keep it. He gave me four pairs of spikes at the beginning of the year. And look. See this shirt? Mickey gave it to me." Adds Shecter, "There has never been a rookie in a Yankee camp who wasn't made to feel a part of the scene by accidentally becoming involved in a kidding chat with Mantle."

But who is Mickey Mantle?

There is the Mickey Mantle who appreciates his fans, but is also intimidated by them. Don't believe the reports that Mickey is indifferent to the fans, especially the kids who worship him. Tom Meany, a baseball writer who once did publicity for the Yankees, tells of the time that Mantle walked into the Yankee office and asked Andy Ryan, who handles the pressroom and assorted duties, for help.

"Mantle handed Ryan a brief clipping he had torn from that morning's New York *Mirror*," said Meany. "It told of the slaying of a boy in Queens by another youth who had been a problem child. The article mentioned that the slain youth had been a Mickey Mantle fan and had been looking forward to a trip to the stadium with his dad, 'so he could see his idol in action.' The story touched Mantle deeply.

" 'Andy,' said Mickey, 'if you could find time this afternoon, I'd like you to write a letter of sympathy to the parents of this boy and bring it to me to sign.' "

And yet this is the Mickey Mantle who is accused of being cold and standoffish, which of course he has to be up to a point lest he be swallowed up by his admirers.

"It's not always easy to be nice," Mantle told writer Shecter in a remarkable interview in *Sport* magazine. "You sign autographs and sign them and then you say 'no more' and you see some little kid put his head down and walk away. I feel sorry for him. But there has to be a stopping point, doesn't there?"

" 'The later arrival of the stopping point, however,' writes Schecter, 'makes a happier man of Mantle, doesn't it?' Mantle grinned his large, nose-crinkling grin, his whole face with the skin so fair it barely tans after a season in the sun, lighting up with it. 'Oh, yea,' he said. 'I'm a lot happier. You know, I used to watch Stan Musial. I'd watch him in spring training and I'd go to his restaurant and watch him there. He's always smiling and real nice. I never saw him mad. He always seems to be happy. People ask him for his autograph and he'd say, Why not? I thought I'd like to be like that. Sometimes I know he doesn't feel like it, but he does it, anyway. It makes a good appearance. I've heard people say, "See that, the biggest men are really nice." I know they mean that I'm not *nice*.' "

But who is Mickey Mantle?

He is nicer than he once was, and he has changed, and he knows that, too. He told Shecter, "I am different now. I care more about what people think about me. It comes easier for me to be nice to people. I feel more comfortable with strangers.

"In the beginning I got messed around quite a bit by a

lot of people. I thought everytime somebody walked up to me there was something they were after and I would be the goat. It's like my wife and I used to go out to dinner and somebody would start over to our table and she would say, 'They're coming over. Now be *nice!*' I can see where I was wrong. I used to embarrass her. It gives you a good feeling to be nice."

Who is Mickey Mantle?

Let's try to find out.

CHAPTER THREE

MUTT'S BOY

The year 1931 was mostly an uneventful year for
the United States. There was a depression and people
were out of work, but it wasn't yet the desperate depression it would become in the mid-1930s. Besides, Herbert
Hoover was President of the United States and prosperity
was just around the corner.

The world itself was mostly at peace (though Mussolini
was making unpleasant noises in Italy). A world disarma-
ment conference was being arranged for 1932. Aviators
Wiley Post and Harold Gatty flew around the world in
record time. The George Washington Bridge was opened
in New York and Thomas Alva Edison, inventor of the

electric light bulb, was dead, on October 18, at age eighty-four.

In sports, forty youngsters were killed playing football and Notre Dame, which had gone undefeated in 1930, went undefeated in 1931—until its last two games, losing then to Southern California and Army. Twenty Grand won the Kentucky Derby, Ellsworth Vines was America's best tennis player and Max Schmeling was the world's heavyweight champion.

And in baseball, the Philadelphia Athletics won the American League pennant by 13 and a half games, but lost a seven-game World Series to the wild Gashouse Gang from St. Louis.

One of the goats of that Series was Athletics' catcher Mickey Cochrane, who batted only .160 and let the Cardinals' Pepper Martin run like Maury Wills on the base paths.

But on October 20, 1931, in an ink blot of a town, Spavinaw, Oklahoma, population 300, Mickey Cochrane was forgiven. That day a newborn was christened Mickey Charles Mantle, the Mickey for the Philadelphia catcher.

The land in that northeast corner of Oklahoma was hard land, and men worked under it to make a living. All around were the "chat" piles, pebbly refuse mounds which came from the lead and zinc that had been extracted from the ore. The chat piles rose like mountains against the sky.

One of the miners in that dry, desolate area of America was a man named Charles Mantle. As a kid he had played lots of baseball. Even as a miner he played baseball, both for money (with semipro teams in the area) and as a release from the relentless drudgery of his work. He was a left-handed pitcher and his son, Elven, grew up to be a right-handed pitcher and played on the same semipro teams as his dad.

But there was never that much baseball for the Mantles. Their life, and the life of most of the people in the neighborhood, revolved around the mines. The Mantle clan was pure Oklahoma, born and bred in that region of the country called the tri-state district because the northeast corner of Oklahoma comes close to the southeast corner of Kansas, and to the southwest corner of Missouri.

Elven Mantle went down into the mines like his dad, but in the back of his mind he cherished an abiding dream—that, some day, one of his own flesh and blood would grow up to be a great professional baseball player and escape the grim life of a miner.

Mutt Mantle ("Mutt" was his nickname) told that dream more than once to the woman he chose to marry, a tall, spirited young lady named Lovell Richardson. And Lovell allowed how it would be wonderful if it could work out that way.

Mutt Mantle not only played ball, he followed the big-leaguers, too, He favored no particular team but he took quite a liking to Mickey Cochrane. In 1929 Cochrane batted .331 for the Athletics, and the next year he batted .357 In 1931 while a teammate, Al Simmons, was hitting .390 and leading the American League, Cochrane batted a respectable .349. And by then everyone figured him as the best catcher in baseball.

This was good enough for the twenty-year-old Mutt who, when informed that his wife was carrying their first child, told her, "If it's a boy, we're gonna name him Mickey, after Mickey Cochrane."

In those early months of the boy's first year, Elven and his father kept a close eye on the offspring. They talked to each other more than once about what kind of an athlete the baby would turn out to be. As if to help matters along, when Mickey was six months old, Mutt ordered his wife to make a baseball cap to fit the baby's head. And two and a half years later, Mutt had his wife tailor a complete uniform for the boy—using Mutt's own uniform pants. Mickey doesn't remember when he got his first glove, but he does remember that it was a Joe Gordon model.

When Mickey was four years old, the family took up from Spavinaw and moved 70 miles to Commerce, a town with a population of 2,500. Now there were twin boys in the family, Roy and Ray, and Mutt found a better job as ground boss in the Blue Goose No. 1 lead and zinc mine of the Eagle-Picher Mining Company.

Much of Commerce is built over the mines, and that included Mantle's home. Mickey once told a visitor, "You know, there's a mine right under the chair you're sittin' in. Three hundred feet down the men are working in the ground."

The family moved into a clapboard house at 319 Quincy Street. There was a large backyard, where Mickey's father and grandfather could begin the boy's apprenticeship as a baseball player.

Mickey began Central Grade School when he was six and that was when he began a parallel education in baseball. When Mickey returned from school one day he met his father and grandfather out in the backyard. They had a small bat and some tennis balls and Mickey looked at them wonderingly.

Mutt came up to his son holding the bat.

"You take this bat," Mutt said, "and just try to hit the balls we throw you. We won't throw them hard, so don't worry about getting hurt."

Mickey took the bat and he swung at the air. It was a smooth, natural, right-handed swing for Mickey. He was a right-hander all the way.

"Now there's one thing I want to tell you," Mutt said. "When I throw the ball, you go ahead and swing the way you're doing it now. But when Grandpa Charley throws the ball, I want you to turn around and swing the other way. Understand?"

Mickey did not quite understand, but he did what he was told, anyway. He could not understand that Mutt Mantle was trying to give his son an advantage. Tom Greenwade, the scout who signed Mickey, once said, "Mutt Mantle knew more about baseball than the father of any boy I ever signed."

Mutt knew that it would be to Mickey's advantage to switch-hit. Against a left-handed pitcher, a right-handed batter is better off than a left-handed batter because the curve ball breaks in toward him and he can follow it better with his eyes. Against a right-handed pitcher, a left-handed batter has the edge for the same reason—plus the fact that he can speed down the first-base line faster than if he were standing right-handed at the plate. The best time to develop a batter as a switch-hitter, Mutt reasoned, was when a boy was very young.

He was right, of course, but in those early days—Mutt

pitching left-handed, Grandfather Charley pitching right-handed and Mickey dutifully swinging from both sides of the plate—the young boy was not too happy about his father's theory.

At first, Mickey just didn't like it at all. He felt unnatural swinging from the left side of home plate, and he tried on occasion to swing only righty. Once during a sandlot game, he came to bat right-handed against a right-handed pitcher. His father, who happened to be watching, became very angry. He made Mickey leave the game and go home.

He barked at the boy, "Don't you ever put on that baseball uniform again until you switch-hit like I taught you."

Mickey complained once or twice to his mother about switch-hitting, but she was on her husband's side. "You do what your father says," ordered Mrs. Mantle. "Some day you'll be glad you listened to your father."

The days went by slowly at first for the six-year-old. He would get home from school about 3:30, change into his old clothes, practice until it got dark in the evening. On rare occasions when his dad was satisfied that the boy was learning, he would give Mickey an off day to go hunting or fishing. The young Oklahoman loved those sports.

But mostly it was hard work, swinging a bat from both sides of the plate, with the two devoted instructors taking turns throwing to the boy. Soon, Mickey Mantle began to get the hang of hitting left-handed, and he lost his awkwardness and started blasting the ball left-handed as well as he always did right-handed.

It went on like that past the school season, to the summer. There were days when Mickey would stay out four or five hours just hitting the ball. Mutt and Charley began throwing curves to Mickey and Mickey began hitting the twisting gyrations of that tennis ball almost as well as he hit the fast pitch.

After a year, the tennis ball was replaced by the baseball. But to make it more fun for Mickey, his dad devised a scheme. A ground ball, a pop fly, a strikeout, were outs. A line drive past the pitcher was a single, off the house a double, off the roof a triple and into the next lot a home run. Mickey hit plenty of home runs in those early days, and as his skill improved, so did his determination to become a big league ballplayer.

Soon baseball became the biggest thing in his life. When he wasn't practicing with his dad and grandfather, he was talking baseball or listening to the radio broadcasts of Cardinal games. By the time he was ten, Mickey's schoolmates were already joking about his dedication to the game. "When it comes 4 in the afternoon," the jest went, "Mickey has to stop playing baseball and start practicing the game."

It was in his eleventh year that Mickey first became involved with organized ball. It was as a ninety-pound catcher for the Douthat, Oklahoma team in the Pee Wee League. Mickey was the only switch-hitter in the league. He was also the league's best hitter, though his catching could have been improved on.

"When he squatted down behind the bat," his mother recalled, "wearing that protector that was too big for him, you couldn't see his feet and about all you could see of him except for his arms were those two little eyes sticking out of the protector like a scared turtle looking out of its shell."

Yet Mickey became one of the Pee Wee League's best

ballplayers. He could hit farther than anyone, and he also had more drive than the other boys. "When he got a single," a Commerce neighbor recalled, "he would come back to the bench muttering, 'It should have been a double.' "

Mickey helped Douthat to the league championship and, after that, the teams he played on always won championships. He didn't play with a loser until the 1954 Yankees, who were nosed out of the American League pennant by the Cleveland Indians.

The next year Mickey graduated to the Commerce-Picher Gabby Street team, and Mutt Mantle permitted his son to be switched from catcher—Mickey Cochrane's position, remember—to shortstop. But by this time, Mickey's dad had other things on his mind.

He had moved his family—which now consisted of Mickey, the twins, a daughter Barbara and a younger son, Larry—to the outskirts of Commerce. Grandfather Charley had become sick and Mutt, in order to get him away from the mines, had bought some chickens, cows, hogs and a tractor and tried farming on 180 acres along the Neosho River.

It was a gamble on Mutt's part, but for the kids it was a holiday. "It made it a lot easier to hunt and fish," Mickey once recalled. "I rode a horse to school, which was about ten miles away. He sure was an understanding horse. He didn't like school, either. He loved to run away with me on his back and start grazing around some fishing hole."

Mutt Mantle had bad luck with his farm. During one terrible rainy spell, the Neosho River overflowed and ruined the corn, wheat and oats that Mutt had planted. He went bankrupt and the Mantles moved back to Com-

merce. Mutt went back to work in the mines. Grandfather
Charles died in 1945.

Meanwhile, Mickey had begun to establish his reputation in the area as a baseball phenomenon. Playing two
seasons in the Gabby Street League, mostly against boys
several years older than himself, Mickey was the star of
the league.

In 1945, the year his grandfather died and Mickey was
fourteen, he entered Commerce High School as a fresh-
man. He played basketball and informal baseball that first
year (the school was class B, not big enough to have a
regular team). That summer Mickey played in the Junior
Cardinal League, which was affiliated with American Le-
gion baseball.

In the fall of 1946, Mickey went out for football. His
dad wasn't very happy about it. Mutt Mantle wasn't afraid
for Mickey. But he did fear that a football injury could
ruin Mickey's chances in baseball. But Mickey pleaded
and his father, realizing the extent of the boy's desire,
gave in.

Mutt's worst fears were realized almost at once.

It happened that first fall of organized football for
Mickey. He had been running at halfback with the first
team and his coaches knew they had a good one. One
afternoon, during a preseason scrimmage, Mickey was
carrying the ball through the line. In a big pile-up, a
teammate accidentally kicked Mickey in the left ankle.
Mickey continued to play, but after practice the pain
became much worse.

At home that night the boy was unable to sleep. In the
morning he took one look at the leg and became frightened. The ankle was blue and blown up twice its normal

size and was loaded with pus. Mutt Mantle rushed his son to the local doctor.

The doctor examined the ankle carefully and prescribed a certain treatment. But when the ankle began to get worse, Mickey's coach at Commerce High, Allen Woolard, called Mutt Mantle. "I think you should have Mickey see this bone specialist in Picher, and I wouldn't waste any time."

Mutt Mantle rushed his son to Picher where the bone specialist carefully examined the ankle and took X-rays. A little while later, he took Mutt Mantle aside.

"Your son has a bone disease," said the doctor. "It's called osteomyelitis."

"What does that mean?" Mutt asked.

"Osteomyelitis," replied the doctor, "is a bone infection. It produces chronic inflammation of the bones. We can treat it and help it, but we can't cure it."

"You mean, he'll always have it?" Mutt was staggered by the doctor's explanation.

"With treatment," said the doctor, "the pain and swelling will disappear. But it could come back. It could come back even if your son bruises the leg slightly."

"My son is a ballplayer," Mutt Mantle said slowly, "a good ballplayer. What do you suggest I do?"

"I would go to Oklahoma City. They have the latest medical facilities. They can help you the most."

So Mutt and Mickey picked up and drove to Oklahoma City. Mickey was there two weeks. The ankle was lanced and Mickey was given penicillin injections every three hours. At first, the ankle failed to respond to the treatment and the doctors actually considered the possibilities of amputation. But, finally, the swelling subsided. The disease had been arrested.

Mickey returned to Commerce on crutches in September 1946. He was an unhappy young man. He felt his whole world had turned upside down. What would he do now if he could never play sports again? Mutt Mantle felt almost as bad and to cheer his son up, he splurged on two tickets to the opening games of the 1946 World Series in St. Louis, 300 miles from Commerce.

Those were the first two major league games Mickey had ever seen and he was happy and excited watching the Red Sox and Cardinals go at each other. He saw the Sox win the opening game, 3–2, on a tenth inning home run by Rudy York. Then he saw his favorite team, the Cardinals, come back in the second game, 8–0, on Harry Brecheen's four-hitter.

He returned to Commerce in a better state and listened to the rest of the Series on the radio. He let out a big whoop when, in the eighth inning of the last game, the score tied 3–3, Enos Slaughter scored all the way from first on Harry Walker's hit over the shortstop's head. Of course he had no idea that one day he, Mickey Mantle, the boy from Oklahoma, would be playing side by side in the same outfield with Enos Slaughter, the hero of the 1946 World Series.

Mickey went back to school, tossed away his crutches and played basketball for Commerce High. And in the spring he was well enough to play baseball again.

In the fall of 1947 Mickey went out for football again, but the coaches handled him gingerly. It wasn't until his senior year that he played football full-time—and what a player he was! He was used as a halfback in the T-formation and a fullback in the single wing and he scored ten touchdowns in seven games. "He would have made a great T-quarterback," says his high school coach, John Lingo. Lingo felt that Mantle could easily have gotten a football scholarship to the college of his choice.

"He made All-District his senior year," Lingo remembered. "And he got better with every game. One game we played Miami and Mickey punted for the first time and he kicked it over the safety man's head. He could pass, too. We had another fine passer on that team, fellow name of Bill Mosley. Mickey threw a harder pass than Mosley but the boys always told me Mickey's seemed hard but wasn't, even though he threw it like a bullet.

"I was kind of glad nobody sought out Mickey for college football. I knew he would have to wrestle with his preferences and I also knew his dad would have been heartbroken if a chance came along for professional baseball and Mickey wasn't in a position to take it. Heck, Mickey could have made it just as big in basketball. We used him as a guard. We never did see anybody ever get the ball away from him."

Ralph Terry, the Yankee pitcher, who grew up in nearby Chelsea, Oklahoma, was three years behind Mickey in school. He agrees with Lingo. He says that Mickey had a terrific high school reputation but that basketball was his best sport. "Mickey was a great shot and a terrific playmaker," Ralph remembers.

But it was still baseball for Mickey. He knew how his dad felt about the game, and Mickey loved it, too, more than any other sport. And he was getting better and better.

In his junior year at Commerce High, the school finally

organized a baseball team, and of course Mickey was the
star. And because he was the best player, he alternated
between shortstop and pitcher. He didn't have much of a
fast ball but his father showed him how to throw a jug-
handle curve and in one game in the "Lucky Seven
League," as it was called, Mickey struck out 14 players.

In his senior year, Mickey really blossomed as a batter.
In one game against Miami (Oklahoma) Junior College,
he hit home runs left-handed and right-handed. "Mickey
was absolutely no good for us," his coach remembered,
"because the opposition knew all about him. So when he
would come to the plate, they would walk him. He helped
a little in exhibition games against junior colleges. They'd
pitch to him when nobody was on base and two were out."

Meanwhile, Mickey was also playing ball outside, and
this is where he flashed his potential to people in a position to help him. In 1946 he was playing for Miami in the
Ban Johnson League, a rugged amateur league still operat-
ing in the tri-state area and *still* sending ballplayers to the
major leagues. One day late in the season, Miami played
the tough Baxter Springs Whiz Kids, who were managed
by Barney Barnett, a fellow mine hand and an old friend
of Mutt Mantle's.

But friendship was forgotten this day, especially at that
moment late in the game when Mickey Mantle came to
the plate with the bases loaded, nobody out.

Barnett waved in his right fielder. He knew Mickey hit
farther right-handed, and he figured Mickey wouldn't
drive the ball far batting left. On the first pitch, Mickey
swung at a fast ball and sent a low liner screaming out
over second base. But the right fielder, in perfect position,
moved in two steps and picked off the ball at his knees,

then threw to the shortstop. The shortstop turned it into a triple play.

But that smoking hot drive had impressed Barnett. After the game, he came over to Mutt Mantle, who had been watching.

"I'd like Mickey to play for the Whiz Kids next year, Mutt," Barnett said.

"If it's okay with Mickey, it's okay with me," said Mutt.

"I know you got the big leagues figured for him," said Barnett, "and I think you're figuring right. Maybe I can help."

Barney Barnett was figuring right, too.

CHAPTER FOUR

GREENWADE'S DISCOVERY

In June of 1948, Mickey Mantle, not yet seventeen years of age, began to play for Barney Barnett's Baxter Springs Whiz Kids. He was then called "Little Mickey Mantle." He stood five feet eight inches tall, weighed about 165 pounds and had a round, open baby face. But his appearance was slightly misleading. As a batter, even then, Little Mickey Mantle was far from little.

Right off, he became the star of the Whiz Kids and that summer a Ban Johnson League umpire, Kay Jacobson, who was also a fireman from Commerce, tipped off a big league scout about Mantle.

The scout's name was Tom Greenwade, a spare, hatchet-faced gentleman who worked for the New York Yankees. In the past Greenwade had done some important scouting jobs for other teams. It was Greenwade who first recommended Jackie Robinson to Brooklyn Dodger president Branch Rickey.

One day in August of 1948, Greenwade was in the area and he stopped in to see Jacobson.

"They've got a good kid playing in Baxter Springs," Jacobson said. "His name is Mickey Mantle."

"How good?" asked Greenwade.

"He plays shortstop," said Jacobson, "and makes a lot of errors. But he's got a big arm, he's terrifically fast on the bases and he switch-hits—hits as good right-handed as he does left-handed."

"Where can I see him?"

"Come over to Alba [Missouri] tomorrow. The Whiz Kids are playing there."

So Greenwade got his first look at Mantle. He was unimpressed. Mickey played shortstop, made a couple of errors, didn't hit the ball well. He also pitched a few innings, but showed Greenwade nothing. Besides, the Yankee scout had become intrigued with the Whiz Kids' third baseman, Billy Johnson.

After the game, Jacobson asked Greenwade, "What about Mantle?"

"I like that Johnson kid on third," Greenwade said. "Mantle?"

"He's kind of a bitty thing, not too much to see," said Greenwade. "But keep me posted on him."

By this time Mickey had dissolved his allegiance to the Cardinals. He had become a Yankee fan, and since he was trying to make it at shortstop, Yankee shortstop Phil

Joe DiMaggio, the famous "Yankee Clipper," enjoys a light moment with the young Mantle in 1951. DiMaggio was one of many who regarded the rookie from Oklahoma as the replacement for the Yank's great center fielder.

Rizzuto was his hero. But Mickey was far from a Rizzuto at short. Barney Barnett, the Whiz Kids' manager, worked patiently with Mickey, but Mickey just had trouble picking up the ball. He usually managed to block a ground ball hit at him, and he had a tremendous arm, which got him out of a lot of trouble. But he lacked the finesse and quick agility needed to become a first-class shortstop.

Mickey went back to Commerce High for his senior year, starred in football, basketball and baseball. In his high school class yearbook, *Bengal Tales,* there is a caption underneath Mickey's picture that reads:

MICKEY MANTLE

THEY'RE GREAT PALS,

HE AND HIS BASEBALL JACKET.

The first time Jacobson caught up with Mantle in the spring of 1949, at an early Ban Johnson League game, he hardly recognized the boy. Boy? He had grown two inches and put on twenty pounds and already he had that great 17-inch bull neck.

"You've grown up some," Jacobson told Mickey. "Have you given any thought to a baseball career?"

Mickey grinned. "I've done nothing else."

Jacobson said, "I believe you can make it. I want you to go to Joplin and see Johnny Sturm there. He manages the Yankee farm. Ask him to look you over. If he gives you the OK, you'll be on your way."

A couple of days later Mickey hooked a ride with a friend to Joplin, 33 miles from Commerce. He had his glove with him and his baseball shoes. He went in to see Sturm, who had played first base for the Yankees in 1941.

Mickey said shyly, "Mr. Jacobson sent me."

"I know," smiled Sturm. "We've got a uniform for you."

For two nights Mickey worked out at shortstop. He also hit in batting practice against Joplin's Class C pitchers. After the sessions were over, Sturm questioned Mantle.

"When do you finish high school?"

"In about two weeks."

"You looked good out there. Go on home now. You'll hear from us."

Mickey wanted to ask Sturm a lot of questions. Would the Yankees sign him? Could he play shortstop? Could he play Class C ball? Was he really any good? He wanted to ask these and many more questions, but he was scared. He went home still wondering about himself and his chances.

Two weeks later Tom Greenwade came back into Mantle's life.

Greenwade dropped in one day to check on prospects and Sturm and the Joplin business manager, Roy Beavers, both spoke enthusiastically about Mantle.

"The kid's really got possibilities," Sturm said.

"I agree," said Beavers. "He could be a real good one."

"I'll go over and take another look," Greenwade said.

But the Yankees weren't the only club that had heard about Mantle. Runt Marr, a Cardinal scout in the Kansas-Oklahoma-Missouri territory, knew all about Mickey. One day he dropped into the office of Mantle's high school coach, John Lingo.

"I'd like you to take me over to the Mantle house and introduce me to the folks," Marr said.

"Sure," Lingo said. But Lingo also had heard from Greenwade. Tom had called wanting to know when

Mantle would be playing next for the Whiz Kids. Lingo had told the Yankee scout that Baxter Springs would be playing at Coffeyville, Kansas, on May 16. But Mickey wasn't going to play. It was his graduation night.

"I'd love to see him play," Greenwade had said to Lingo.

"I'll see what I can do," said Lingo. So Lingo spoke with Albert Stewart, the superintendent of schools. Stewart knew the stakes for Mickey and he graciously gave Mickey his diploma on the morning of graduation.

Cardinal scout Runt Marr looked in at the Mantles' the day before graduation but only Mickey was home. They didn't have much to say to each other, especially when Mickey said he was a Yankee fan, and very anxious to play with the Yankees. Marr said, "Maybe I'll come back and talk to your pa."

The next day Greenwade came into Commerce, stopped in to see Lingo, who took him to the Mantles' home. There, Tom met Mickey's mother and father, and Mickey.

"The boy's grown," he said to Mutt.

"In more ways than one," said Mutt.

Greenwade, Lingo, Mutt and Mickey Mantle all piled into the scout's car for the trip to Coffeyville, where Mickey would be on display.

They got there early in the afternoon of May 16, 1949. Greenwade dropped Mickey Mantle off with Lingo near a diner in Coffeyville. "Mutt and I are going to take a little ride," he said. "You get something to eat. We'll see you later."

So while Tom Greenwade drove Mantle around, romancing him about the virtues of his son gaining a Yankee education, Mickey and John Lingo sat in the diner. Mickey was nervous and he fussed with the menu.

"What should I order?" he asked.

Lingo said, "Might as well have your usual pregame meal."

"Okay," Mick said to the waitress, "give me a hamburg, French fries and a large glass of milk."

Mickey's nervousness evaporated once the game got under way and though he looked a little uncertain in the field, he was loose at bat. With Greenwade watching and making mental notes, Mickey slammed a triple, double and single in four times up. Lingo, who was sitting next to Greenwade and bursting with curiosity, asked the Yankee scout, "What do you think?"

"I think," Greenwade said, "that I've seen enough."

But after the game, Greenwade made no move to sign the boy. Mutt Mantle, who had built his dreams step by step for almost twenty years, swallowed hard. Hadn't his boy looked like a prospect to the scout?

"Whiz Kids are playing Coffeyville again Sunday, at Baxter Springs," Mutt said. "Maybe you ought to watch them then."

"I'll be there," Tom said.

It was an anxious and uncertain weekend for the Mantles. Mickey could hardly wait for Sunday to come, hoping to cement any good impressions he had made on Greenwade, and correct any bad impressions. He was anxious. Mrs. Mantle was anxious for her husband. Mutt Mantle just curled up anxiously and kept his thoughts to himself. The other Mantle kids felt the tension building in the air—and they were anxious, too.

It was a warm, humid, cloudy night in Baxter Springs when the Whiz Kids took the field against Coffeyville. The air hung heavily over the diamond. Greenwade sat next to Mutt Mantle. Mickey came to bat in the first inning. The pitcher was Carl Pevehouse, a southpaw. Mickey stood up right-handed. It was the first time Greenwade had seen Mickey bat right.

"He do that all the time?" Greenwade asked, forgetting what Kay Jacobson had told him a year earlier.

"All the time," said Mutt, "since he was as high as my knee."

Mickey singled over the shortstop's head. Greenwade mumbled to himself.

He played a good game and just as it was ending, it started to rain. Mutt and Mickey took shelter in Tom's car. Mickey's uniform was damp and stuck to him and his face was beaded with sweat.

Greenwade looked at him and smiled. "You look like a ballplayer at least." Mickey grinned shyly and dropped his head.

"I think you'll be all right, boy," Greenwade said, patting Mickey on the head. Mutt grinned a little, then started to open his mouth. Greenwade stopped him.

"I can sign him to a Class D contract for $140 a month," he said.

Mutt frowned. "Tom, he can make more than that in the mines. He can make eighty-seven and a half cents an hour and play once a week at Spavinaw for fifteen dollars a game."

"Let's see then," Tom said. He took an envelope out of his pocket (inside the envelope was a Yankee contract). He began scrawling figures on it.

"Here's what I can do," he showed Mutt. "I can give him an $1100 bonus and $140 a month as salary for the remainder of the season. That comes to $1450. Any more and he has to be classified as a bonus baby. We'll put him with Independence after a week or so at Branson, Missouri, to watch him a bit."

"What about next year?" asked Mutt.

"If he can handle Class D, we'll try him at Joplin next year," Greenwade said, "close to home."

"How do you feel about it, son?" asked Mutt.

Mickey looked at his dad. "If you feel it's all right, then it's all right with me."

And so it was done. In a parked automobile, in a small town of Midwest America, the dream was fulfilled for the father.

The Yankees? They had made themselves one of the most fabulous deals in their history. When bonus boys were being signed for $75,000 and $100,000, the Yankees had picked off the prize of prizes for a pittance. They had picked off the boy who would one day be placed alongside Ruth, Gehrig and DiMaggio, who would one day be the most explosive and most popular ballplayer of his day.

Tom Greenwade didn't appreciate the full significance of his coup that rainy afternoon in that parked car, but it wasn't long before he realized what he had done.

In the spring of 1950, when Mickey had barely begun his fabulous career, Greenwade sat down with a reporter and talked about young Mantle.

He said, "I've come up with a kid who in a couple of years will be the greatest thing in baseball. His name is Mickey Mantle. When I saw him for the first time, I knew how Paul Krichell felt when he saw Lou Gehrig. Krichell told me once that the first time he saw Gehrig, he knew that as a scout he'd never have another moment in life like it."

Greenwade leaned over and slapped the reporter on the knee. "And you know," he said piously, "I felt the same way when I saw Mantle."

CHAPTER FIVE

EXPRESSWAY
TO THE YANKEES

Ten days after signing his contract, Mickey bid his family good-bye. He was on his way to Branson, Missouri, a Yankee tryout camp, where he would have a few days of instruction and indoctrination. Then on to Independence, Missouri, the Yankees' Class D farm team in the Kansas-Oklahoma-Missouri league.

Mickey arrived at Branson on June 6, 1949. He was immediately taken in hand by a couple of tough old-timers, Dutch Zwilling and Burleigh Grimes. Grimes was an ex-National League spitball pitcher.

"I went up there to learn a few things," Mantle remembered, "and they sure taught me a lot."

Courtesy, *Sport* Magazine

A worried Joe DiMaggio races to Mantle after the rookie fell hard while chasing a ball deep in the outfield.

A few of the little subtleties of professional baseball were drummed into the young boy's head by men like Zwilling and Grimes. It was an eye-opening six-day cram course, and then Mickey was off to Independence, which was 75 miles from Blue Goose No. 1 mine, where Mutt Mantle worked as a ground boss.

But now Mickey Mantle was on his own.

The rest of that 1949 season was a mixture of the good and the not so good. On the one hand, Mickey did some very promising things, at bat and in the field. On the other hand, he also made many mistakes. That was natural, but what disturbed manager Harry Craft was Mickey's lackadaisical attitude. Craft, a former Cincinnati player who later managed Kansas City in the American League, was a hustling ballplayer in his own right and he expected his ballplayers to be hustlers. Mickey, then, was not a hustling ballplayer.

Playing shortstop for Independence, Mickey had 121 putouts and 245 assists in 89 games. But he also committed 47 errors, which gave him an unsatisfactory .886 fielding average.

As a batter, he was much better. His first ten days in an Independence uniform, Mickey was unable to buy a base hit. Craft was thinking of benching him for awhile, but in his 11th game, Mickey lashed out his first hit. From then on, he was a solid batter. He finished with a .313 batting average, 101 singles, 15 doubles, seven triples, seven home runs and 63 runs batted in. It was good enough for a first-year man in organized baseball, especially since Independence went on to win the pennant and play-offs in the K-O-M League. But there were those other problems.

Whenever Mickey made an error or struck out or did something he shouldn't, he would walk back to the dugout, head down, with a sheepish, hangdog look on his face. This made Harry Craft mad.

"Straighten up," he would yell at Mickey. "Nobody is going to arrest you because you made an error. Look at the big league box scores and you'll see that some clubs committed more errors than we did."

Craft urged Mickey to show more hustle—the importance of running at top speed on every ball he hit. "See how many bases you can reach before a pop-up is caught— or dropped or misjudged," Craft suggested.

The manager was driving Mickey hard because he realized the kid's vast potential. At the season's end, Craft sent an enthusiastic report on Mantle to the Yankees' front office.

"Can be a great hitter," the report read. "Exceptional speed. Just an average shortstop. Has a fine arm and a good pair of hands. Let's the ball play him too much. Attitude excellent. Will go all the way. He has everything to make a great ballplayer. I would like to see him shifted to third or the outfield."

Years later, Harry Craft looked back on those days and made a further assessment of the young Mantle. "He could hit," Craft said, "but he had plenty to learn even though he learned fast. It was obvious he was never going to be a really good shortstop. He made too many errors, particularly throwing, even though he had a strong arm. But his real weakness was his temperament. He acted as if the whole world was coming to an end just because he booted one or struck out in the clutch."

That was 1949, when Mickey Mantle was not yet eighteen years old. But the years don't change things that much. Mickey Mantle today is still temperamental, though more subdued than when he was a green young kid scratching towards the majors. The Mickey Mantle of today still gets down on himself when he fails in a clutch situation. He still lets off steam in public. But he has to react this way or burst inside. It was as his mother said some years after he had made the majors. She was sitting in her living room in Commerce talking about her son with Mickey at her side.

"You were never satisfied, were you," Mrs. Mantle said looking straight at her son. "If you got a single, you wanted a double. If, in high school, you struck out 15, you wanted to strike out 16. Now it's still the same."

Mickey got angry listening to his mother. "Ma," he said, "now I got to ask you something. That's the way Pa wanted it, wasn't it?"

"Yes, son," Mrs. Mantle said. "That's the way Pa wanted it."

"Then that's the way I want it," Mickey said, "and I won't be satisfied until that's the way it is."

Mickey celebrated his eighteenth birthday that October of 1949 with his ma and pa back in Commerce. He took a job as an electrician's helper in Blue Goose No. 1, the same mine as his dad.

All that fall and winter, working deep in the bowels of the earth, Mickey's mind was far away from Commerce, Oklahoma, and the mines. He dreamed of baseball, and his future with the Yankees. And he also wondered, with some anxiety, whether he would be good enough to make it—whether he would ever be good enough to be a Yankee.

But those long winter days were made shorter by a few things. In his time-off, Mickey went out and did a lot of hunting. He was especially fond of hunting rabbits in the snow. Later, when he became a Yankee, he would tell his teammates how he used to chase rabbits back in Commerce.

"I'd be fair to them," Mickey would say with a straight face. "I'd chase them in the snow and wouldn't wear spikes or sneakers, and I'd give 'em a fair start."

One November Saturday afternoon, when Mickey had an off-day from work, he and a friend went to a high school football game between Picher and Farland. Each had a date. The friend's date was Merlyn Johnson, a pretty Picher drum majorette. Merlyn at that time had a bigger reputation than Mickey. She sang solo at the First Baptist Church in Picher, and she also sang at nearby Army camps.

A few days later Mickey went over to Picher. He had a date with a girl friend of Merlyn's. Three couples, triple-dating, drove out in the country. The two other boys horsed around and kidded but Mickey was very quiet. Once in a while, though, Merlyn caught his eye, and he grinned at her.

That night after the date Mickey came home and exclaimed not about his girl, but about Merlyn. He told his mother, "I met the cutest little thing in Picher. She twirls one of the batons for the Picher band. She's got freckles, reddish hair and is no taller than that."

The next day Merlyn got a telephone call from her sister Pat's boy friend. "Mickey Mantle wants a date with you," the boy said. Merlyn was a little annoyed that Mickey hadn't called himself, but she agreed. After three dates, Merlyn became Mickey's steady. "I don't know how they ever got acquainted," Merlyn's mother said several years later. "Neither of them ever said a word."

Mickey's anxiety about his baseball future lifted a bit when, in January of 1950, he received a letter from New York. It was from Lee MacPhail, director of the Yankees' farm system.

Mickey tore open the letter eagerly. Would Mickey Mantle like to attend a special school in February at Phoenix, Arizona, a school for the Yankees' best minor league prospects? The Yankees' manager, Casey Stengel, would be there, as well as coaches Bill Dickey, Frank Crosetti and Jim Turner. Such players as Yogi Berra, Tommy Henrich and Hank Bauer would be serving as instructors.

Mickey scrawled a hurried answer: I'll be there.

It was a wondrous time for Mickey Mantle, that first contact with flesh-and-blood major-leaguers. Mantle remembers Casey Stengel addressing the boys the first day in camp. "You fellers all got a chance if you learn something here," Casey said.

One who made the most of that chance was Mantle. Bill Dickey was especially impressed. "I was pitching batting practice when the kid came to the plate," Dickey told writer Tom Meany. "The boy hit the first six balls nearly 500 feet, over the lights and out of sight. He hit them over the fence right-handed and left-handed, and he hit them over the right-field fence right-handed and the left-field fence left-handed.

"When Mantle was playing short, he didn't impress me as being particularly fast, but when we divided the boys up for a series of 75-yard sprints, Mickey finished first in his group, looking over his shoulder at the others. Then we had a sprint for the winners and he won that, too. Then he got sick and explained that he wasn't in shape!

"I honestly believe," Dickey said, "that Mantle is the fastest man I've ever seen in a baseball uniform. I always picked Ben Chapman [the old Yankee outfielder] as the fastest, but I think Mickey could have outrun Ben."

Casey saw Mantle win one of those races one afternoon and he addressed Mickey directly for the first time.

"You just keep chasing those jack rabbits," Stengel said, "and you'll get somewhere. If it's one thing the Yankees can use more of, it's more and better base runners. Now you take the game we lost to Detroit last year. If one of my fellers had run to third the way he was supposed to, we woulda made it a lot easier to win the pennant. I know we didn't win the pennant until the last day of the season, but if we'd won the day I'm talking about, I'd have had my pitchers fresh for the other team and I coulda changed my lineup and it woulda been a lot easier."

Mickey was a little bewildered by this first contact with pure Stengelese, but he nodded obediently and listened as Casey droned on. "Son, if you ever learn how to bunt from either side with that speed, you ought to hit .400. I like you young fellas, like to play 'em in the big leagues when they're supposed to be too young to play in the big leagues. Now you go back out there on the field and keep practicing what they're teaching you."

Mickey did as he was told. But after only two weeks at

the camp, baseball commissioner Happy Chandler said the Yankees were jumping the gun on spring training and he ordered the camp closed.

So Mickey went back to Commerce. But he had one consolation. The Yankees invited Mickey to train with the Kansas City team in the Class AAA American Association—the Yankees' highest farm team.

At Lake Wales, Florida, Mickey worked hard in the few weeks he spent with Kansas City. But then he was assigned to join Joplin, Missouri, in the Class C Western Association, just as scout Tom Greenwade had promised Mickey and his dad a year earlier.

"I'll tell you how good that kid was at Joplin," Greenwade reminisced to a reporter. "One day I'm talking to the manager of the Enid, Oklahoma, team and he says to me: 'We had pretty good luck with this kid last night. He got four hits, but they were all singles.'"

Halfway through the season Mickey was batting .414 for Joplin. He tapered off a bit, ending the 1950 season with a .383 batting average, tops in the league. He scored 141 runs, also tops in the league. He got 199 hits, also tops. Fifteen of those hits were bunts. Of his 26 home runs, 14 were hit right-handed, 12 were hit left-handed. He drove in 126 runs. Joplin won the pennant and Mickey earned the $250 a month they were paying him.

He also got $2.25 a day for meals that year and he remembered that there were two bats for the whole team. "One was a Chuck Klein model," Mickey said, "and the other a Harry Craft model. If one of them got broken, we just had to do the best we could with the other until we could send to the store and buy a new one."

All in all, it was a tremendous year for the eighteen-year-old Commerce comet. But it was not without its strains.

Moving up to Joplin with Mantle was manager Harry Craft, who continued to drive his star hard. He worked on Mantle's batting swing, his base running, his fielding and his general baseball knowledge. He worked, too, to curb Mantle's temper. Once, when Mickey threw his bat after a strikeout, Craft hollered, "Stop throwing the bat or I'll bench you."

By this time Mickey Mantle was filling out physically. He was a solid five feet 11, weighing 185 pounds. He had powerful arms, back and leg muscles, that all helped add energy to his swing. Dashing around the base paths with his head down and arms pumping, he looked like a sprinter exploding out of starting blocks.

Back in New York all the Yankees—players and executives—had heard about Mantle, all about the exploits of the eighteen-year-old phenomenon who could smash the ball with power from both sides of the plate, who could run like the very wind, who could slide like a Cobb and throw like a DiMaggio. One of the Yankee players most interested in Mantle was Mickey's hero, Yankee shortstop Phil Rizzuto.

"I kept an eye on all the shortstops in the Yankee chain," Phil says, "figuring someday one of them would take my job."

The manager, Casey Stengel, was also much interested. He told his general manager, George Weiss, "Bring Mantle to New York after Joplin finishes its season. Let him work out with us. In actual playing experience, it won't mean nothing to the kid. But it'll get him used to being around big league ball parks. It'll let him get the feel of being with the Yankees."

So early in September, Mickey Mantle prepared to join the Yankees. He would pick up the team in St. Louis, where the Yanks were playing the Browns. Before he left Joplin, Harry Craft called him in for some last words.

"You're going to make a lot of new and influential friends as you advance in baseball," Craft said. "But remember this—don't forget the old ones. They're the ones who made you."

In St. Louis it was a brand-new world for the eighteen-year-old Mantle. He lived in the plush Chase Hotel, ate steaks, rubbed elbows with all these celebrated Yankee heroes—Joe DiMaggio, Vic Raschi, Yogi Berra, Allie Reynolds, Phil Rizzuto. In St. Louis those first days, Mickey stayed shyly in the background, not daring even to take batting practice.

But when his team got to Chicago, another prospect joined the club. His name was Bill Skowron and Mickey and Skowron joined up. They hurried out to the park each day, dressed quickly and put in some batting practice before the regulars reached the field.

In the final days of the Yankees' triumphant year, when they won the pennant and would go on to win the World Series in four straight against the Philadelphia Phillies, the Yankee management brought Mickey's whole family into New York. Mutt Mantle came, his wife Lovell, the twins Roy and Ray, and Mickey's girl friend, Merlyn.

It was a big thrill for the folks to visit Yankee Stadium. When Mutt Mantle met the players, he acted very casual. He told Rizzuto how he had taught his son to switch-hit.

Mantle chats with Mel Allen during the 1954 season. Allen has announced Yankee games over radio and television for many years.

And Casey Stengel complimented Mutt on his baseball know-how. "Maybe I ought to sign you as a coach," Stengel said. Mutt grinned.

The whole family went back to Commerce together, where Mickey went back into the mines—at $33.90 a week take-home pay. And on his off days he dated Merlyn and went out hunting rabbits in the snow.

Mickey now was listed on the roster of the Yankees' Binghamton, Class A team, but he was told to report to the Yankees' training camp at Phoenix. He wasn't sure when, though. Late in January, he got a letter from New York inviting him to the Yankees' Phoenix school two weeks ahead of regular training.

He was due to report on February 15. The day came and Mantle hadn't arrived. General Manager Weiss was disturbed. "That isn't like the boy," he said. "Something must be wrong."

Veteran Tommy Henrich suggested to Weiss, "Maybe he doesn't have the money."

"I'll call and find out," Weiss said.

Mickey received the call at the Blue Goose No. 1 mine. "Where are you?" Weiss asked impatiently. "Why aren't you in Phoenix?"

"I'm broke," Mickey said. "I don't have any money for transportation."

Mickey had used his bonus money to help pay off the mortgage on the Mantles' six-room frame house in Commerce.

Two hours later Mickey got a call from Western Union. The Yankees had wired money and instructions as to which train to catch.

Mickey stuffed his clothes in a suitcase, said good-bye to his family and promised to let them know how he was doing.

Before long, the whole country would know how he was doing.

CHAPTER SIX

"TO WATCH HIM PLAY, GIVES ONE A LIFT"

To most of the Yankee ballplayers, and would-be Yankee ballplayers converging on their Phoenix, Arizona, spring training base, the name Mickey Mantle had no meaning. It was a nice name, a ballplayer's name, but who in heck was Mickey Mantle?

Some people knew.

The general manager, George Weiss, read the Mantle record—at Independence and Joplin—and wondered where he would place the nineteen-year-old. Should it be Binghamton, Class A? Or might it be possible for Mantle to make the big jump, to Kansas City, Class AAA?

The manager, Casey Stengel, who had already caught

some mouth-watering glimpes of Mantle, wondered about the possibility of Mantle sticking with the Yankees in 1951.

The great Yankee Clipper, Joe DiMaggio, who knew that 1951 would be his last season, wondered if Mickey Mantle would be able to help the Yankees by 1952.

The Yankee shortstop, Phil Rizzuto, who in 1950 was voted the American League's Most Valuable Player, wondered about Mickey Mantle, because Mantle too was a shortstop. Phil had always kept a close watch on the shortstops in the Yankee chain, and here was a boy who, in two minor league seasons, had batted .313 the first, .383 the second—and was a power hitter to boot. Phil wondered, and worried.

And on the train heading west, the young ballplayer looked out the window and wondered, too. Watching the landscape blur by, the rookie ballplayer speculated about his chances of one day becoming a Yankee. His speculations varied wildly—full of hope and fantasies, doubt and faint desperation, and also a sense of fate. If things went well, the rookie ballplayer thought to himself, fine. If they didn't, well there were always other things to do besides play baseball. There were always the zinc mines. . . .

What finally happened that spring of 1951 in Phoenix, Arizona, is something that has not often happened before in any major league baseball camp, and has not happened since. Like Aladdin's Genie, Mickey Mantle, the rookie ballplayer, exploded out of a bottle.

He was one of a large group of Yankee hopefuls who had been invited to attend the pre-training instructional school. During the last week of February school let out, but three of the rookies were asked to stay on and work with the Yankees. They were: twenty-three-year-old third baseman Gil McDougald, who had played for Class AA Beaumont in 1950; twenty-one-year-old pitcher Tom Morgan, who had played for Binghamton, Class A; and nineteen-year-old Mickey Mantle, who came from Joplin, Class C baseball.

As the regulars trooped into camp, they began to hear stories about the Mantle boy. They heard about how he had slugged the ball over the center-field fence, which was 430 feet away, how he could bat with impressive power from both sides of the plate. They wanted to know more about the husky, blond, baby-faced young man with the large muscles, the shy grin and the nasal Oklahoma twang to his voice. Mickey himself didn't know what to say to people such as Rizzuto and Yogi Berra and Joe DiMaggio and Jerry Coleman, so they tried to put him at ease. It was Yogi Berra who first cornered Mickey in the Yankee clubhouse.

"Where you from, kid?" Yogi asked.

"Commerce, Oklahoma," Mickey said.

"Hmmmmm," said Yogi. "That near any big city?"

"Miami, Oklahoma," said Mantle. "Got 10,000 people in it."

"Wow!" Yogi said shaking his head and concealing a big grin.

Phil Rizzuto also went up to Mantle and sounded him out a bit. Mickey sensed what Rizzuto was fishing for and put him at ease. "If they put me at shortstop here," Mickey said, "I'll lead the league in errors just as I did the Western League."

Rizzuto, watching the youngster work out at short, felt a little better. He saw that Mantle had an erratic arm for

The camera catches Mantle at the powerful follow through of his swing.

an infielder, and that his instincts were a little slow for a major league shortstop. Casey Stengel saw much the same thing. "His hands aren't quick enough for shortstop," said Stengel. "He's lost on a bad bounce."

And then on March 2, in a historic hotel interview with three sportswriters, Joe DiMaggio told of his plans for retiring. "I want to have a good year and then hang 'em up," DiMag said.

The next morning, Mickey Mantle was moved from shortstop to the outfield, where he was put under the personal supervision of Yankee coach Tommy Henrich.

That was a historic occasion for more than one reason. Mickey played in an intra-squad game, center field for the second team. In the first inning, batting left-handed against right-handed pitcher Wally Hood, Mickey blasted a line drive to the center-field fence. In the second inning he drove a home run over the right-field fence, 350 feet away. Playing cautiously with his back to the palm trees and mountains that rose behind the fences, Mantle made one outfield put-out.

Tommy Henrich, the Old Reliable of the Yankees, one of the best outfielders the Yankees ever had, worked hard on Mickey. All he had was the raw material. Mickey knew nothing about playing the outfield. He didn't know how to use his glasses. He didn't know how to throw from the outfield. He would chase balls hit behind him with his head down. Once Stengel hollered to Mickey to look over his shoulder as he ran back. "This is the big leagues," Casey said. "We don't have no plowed fields for you to run through."

Henrich ran Mickey's legs off hour after hour chasing

fly balls. He taught Mickey how to flip his sunglasses up and down, how to come in on line drives, how to throw from deep in the outfield.

It was a little tough on the kid because he had never played the outfield before. He once explained his feelings about the switch. "There's a lot more to playing the outfield than most people know. But the first day out there, I knew I was going to like it better than the infield. I can run a lot more out there and that's something I always liked to do. I'm still uncertain, but I'm learning. It may take a long time, but I'll master it. I know I will."

Tommy Henrich felt the same way. "I must have hit hundreds of fungoes each day to Mickey," Henrich explained. "He would get to them but his main trouble was that he didn't go back far enough. He wasn't catching the ball in front of him but more or less over his shoulder. That, of course, was bad. I kept reminding him that he had to be in a position to throw the ball."

At the beginning, Mickey was very awkward. In the Yankees' second exhibition game against the Cleveland Indians, Ray Boone hit a line drive to center. Mickey tried to flip his sunglasses down and while tugging at them, lost sight of the ball. He was hit on the forehead by Boone's line drive. But in the Yankees' next game, against the Chicago White Sox, he showed that he had some natural aptitude for the outfield.

Mickey was in right field and Chicago's Jim Busby, a ten-second man, was on third base. The batter hit a long hooking drive to Mantle. Mickey raced back. He caught the ball off his right hip and, all in the same motion, brought his arm around and ripped the throw into the plate. Jim Busby, who had come halfway home, saw the throw zoom in. He scrambled back to third. At the end of the inning coach Henrich came out to greet Mantle.

"Young fella," Tommy said, "I've done a lot of talking to you. Forget all I've said. Just do it the way you did. That's all."

His fielding came along slowly, but his batting was sensational from the beginning. The first time he stepped into the batting cage at Phoenix, veteran ballplayers—even Joe DiMaggio—stopped what they were doing to watch. What they saw was a left-handed slugger blasting balls deep over the right-field fence, then turning around and blasting balls deep over the left-field fence. The Yankee players watched him hit and they watched him run and they all knew that there had to be a spot for Mantle in the lineup.

Casey Stengel said as much to reporters covering the team early that March. "As far as hitting, he's a big-leaguer. The kid is absolutely tremendous. How do you pitch to him? Right-handed? Left-handed? Just when they think they got it solved, the kid smacks one farther than anyone else ever hit it, left- or right-handed."

But Casey was also puzzled about what to do with Mickey. "All I know is that he has me terribly confused and he's getting me more so every day. I know that he's not a big league outfielder yet and that he should have a year of Triple-A ball under his belt. That's the only logical thing. But this kid ain't logical. He's a big league hitter now. He can run the bases and his speed kinda keeps you on edge. His speed is so big that maybe he can use it in the outfield. And his arm is so strong that he won't have to think out there. All he'll have to do is throw the ball in."

Then Casey tried to throw the burden on the sportswriters. "You guys have all blowed him up so much that I have to take him to New York. Don't get me wrong. I'm not blaming you. He's been everything you say he is. He is faster than Cobb. But it doesn't figure that he's ready. Then again, nothing he does figures. He's too good. It's very confusing."

It *was* almost impossible for the normally cynical New York writers to restrain themselves about Mantle. In one hitting drill at Phoenix Municipal Stadium, they saw Mickey come up left-handed and hit the right-center field wall, 360 feet away. The next time he came up righty and cleared the left-field fence. The writers had to put it all down, didn't they?

On March 10, the Yankees opened the exhibition season against the Indians at Tucson. The Yankees lost 6–5 but Mantle playing in center field for DiMaggio, ripped two singles off Early Wynn. And he was off and running. In his first 20 times at bat, Mickey had ten hits—a .500 average. In one game he hit a home run 450 feet over deepest center field. In another game, coming to bat only twice, he stroked a long double off the left-field wall, and next time up he beat out a grounder to the second baseman. Said one camp follower watching Mantle, "I have to tell you he's faster than Cobb. Maybe my memory is tricking me, but I'd have to swear he is."

And his teammates were just as awed. Pitcher Frank Shea said, "He's the only guy I ever saw who could bunt .300 and hit .300. That's .600, ain't it, even though he's only hitting .500 now. I'm giving him a 100-point spread on account of his being a switch-hitter."

Was it any wonder then that the sportswriters covering the Yankees found it difficult to restain their enthusiasms about Mantle? They began comparing Mickey to Mel Ott, who came up to the Giants when he was sixteen, an infant out of Gretna Green, Louisiana, who would cock his right leg and smash at the pitches with the power of a veteran. Manager John McGraw converted Ott from a catcher to an outfielder and Mel never left the Giants. Casey remembered the Ott Cinderella story and he dreamed of doing the same with Mantle.

The Yankees went on a swing through California, and West Coast fans got a close-up glimpse of the phenomenon they had been reading so much about. And they were not disappointed.

At Hollywood's Gilmore Stadium, Mickey had the crowd oohing and aahing in batting practice. Batting left-handed, Mickey hit eight into the boulevard behind the right-field fence. Later, in a game at Wrigley Field in Los Angeles, Mickey smashed a mighty home run. The ball landed against a red brick building in the right-center field bleachers, a spot reached only eight or nine times in the history of the ball park, once by Babe Ruth in an exhibition game.

At Hollywood when the Yankees played the Pirates, an interested spectator was Pirates' owner Branch Rickey. Rickey was anxious to see the nineteen-year-old outfielder everyone was raving about, so that he could professionally cut Mickey down to size. Here is what Rickey saw: Mickey bat left-handed and smash a ball over the right-field wall; Mickey bat left-handed and smash a ball over the left-field wall; Rickey saw a blurred streak going down the first-base line. Branch Rickey saw enough. Late in the game he reached into an inside pocket and tore loose a check from its folder. Theatrically, he signed his name to it and then handed the blank check to Dan Topping, co-owner of the Yankees, who sat beside him.

"With this," said Rickey with a flourish, "I make my official bid to buy Mickey Mantle for the Pirates. Name your own price, but for goodness sake be reasonable."

It is said that Topping's reply was, "The very lowest price would be Ralph Kiner and $500,000." And at that, the Yankee owner was kidding.

Later, in a more serious vein, Rickey said, "I've been looking for ballplayers for a long time and he's the finest prospect I've ever seen. He's my ideal rookie. He's the kind of kid that I always dreamed of finding, but never have. He has the flawless, level swing and the fastest break from the plate I've ever seen."

Joe DiMaggio, talking about Mantle to reporters from his home town in San Francisco, said much the same as Rickey. "He's about the greatest prospect I've ever seen," Joe said. "I can't remember anybody as good as he is at his age. Maybe he still has to learn something about catching a fly ball, but he's a big league hitter right now."

That day in San Francisco, Mickey stole third base and Yankee West Coast scout Joe Devine, sitting in the stands, marveled. "He was 35 feet from the bag," said Devine, "and he took two strides and was in. That means he strides seventeen feet, a good sprinter's stride."

On March 26, playing at the University of Southern California's Bovard Field, Mickey lifted his batting average to .432 with two homers, a triple and an infield single. And he drove in seven runs.

Late in the spring, while there was still some doubt whether Mickey would make the varsity, he injured his wrist. His batting average fell a little. In a game against the Pirates early in April, Mickey's name was not posted in the starting lineup. He went to see Stengel.

Mickey said, "Look, they're using a left-hander. I can hit right-handed. My wrist doesn't bother me when I swing from that side. Let me in there."

"Okay," said Casey, "but out you come when a right-hander goes in. I'm not taking any chances."

Cliff Chambers, a tall, string bean southpaw with plenty of major league experience, faced Mickey in the first inning. He tried to slow-curve Mickey but the youngster lashed a single to left. On the next trip he rocketed a screaming liner that almost tore off Chambers' glove.

In the fifth, Mickey faced a Pirate rookie right-hander, Vernon Law. Casey still didn't want Mickey to hit left-handed, so Mickey compromised. "I'll drag a bunt," he said. He did and if he hadn't stumbled breaking for first, he would have beaten it out.

In the seventh, the Pirates had another left-hander in there and Mickey stroked another single to left. His three hits raised his spring average to .443, with 37 hits including five doubles, five home runs and a triple in 61 trips.

After that game, Yankee coach Jim Turner was positively ecstatic. "He's just the greatest I ever saw," Turner said. "Why you could pitch to Stan Musial when he first came up. But you can't to this kid. The Pirates had heard all about him and they were trying to curve and slow-ball him to death. But it didn't bother him. The way he hit those curves and change-ups—that's the tell, you know. I don't think he saw a fast ball all day.

"Another reason why you gotta like the kid," said Turner, "is the way he studies his trade. You know, he sits up there on the lip of the dugout and he watches the pitcher every second."

Only one question remained to be formally answered. Would the Yankees buy Mantle's contract, or would they send him down for more seasoning? Stengel in public professed to uncertainty about the wisdom of bringing the boy to the varsity without more minor league experience. But privately, his mind was made up—he wanted Mickey with the Yankees. General manager George Weiss, on the other hand, felt that Mantle could use more minor league experience. A normally cautious man, Weiss felt that Mickey would be that much better with a year batting against Triple-A pitching, and a year in which to learn how to play the outfield.

The question nearly became academic because the day after Mickey had that great game against the Pirates, he received a notice from his draft board in Miami, Oklahoma. They wanted Mickey Mantle back for another physical examination.

Mickey had taken his first draft physical in December of 1950 and, because of the osteomyelitis, had been pronounced unfit for military service. But now that Mickey Mantle was a celebrity, people began asking cruel questions. His local draft board received letters. The director of Selective Service, Lewis Hershey, received letters. The President of the United States received letters. All said essentially the same thing. "How come Mickey Mantle can run like a deer and hit like a Babe Ruth and can't serve in the Army?"

Mickey left the Yankees on April 11 for his physical. Three days later an anxious baseball public got the news: Osteomyelitis automatically disqualifies a man for military service. Once again, Mickey was classified 4–F.

He flew back to New York. He had barely slept for seventy-two hours but he was put in the starting lineup against Brooklyn in the last preseason game. Early on Saturday morning at Ebbets Field, home of the Dodgers, Casey Stengel was seen walking out to the right-field fence with Mickey, making gestures. Later, reporters asked Casey what he was doing.

"The boy never saw concrete before," said Casey. "I wanted to show him this wall because he never seen one like it before. I showed him how it starts straight up—down here—like any other wall and then there is this break here and it slants. I tell him how to play the ball glancing off the wall. I say to him: 'I played this wall for six years.' He looks at me like I'm kidding or something and he says, 'You did?' I guess the boy thinks I was born at the age of sixty and right away became a major league manager."

That Saturday game against the Dodgers, Mickey Mantle got only one single. The next day, feeling stronger, Mickey did better. In the first inning, batting right-handed against Joe Hatten, he singled. Later, batting left-handed off Joe Romano, he got two more singles. In the eighth inning up left-handed, he homered over the right-field fence, clearing a 38-foot scoreboard at a position 344 feet from the plate. He had four for five. He finished the exhibition season with 41 hits in 102 times at bat, seven doubles, one triple, 31 runs batted in, nine home runs—a .402 batting average.

That night, the final question was resolved. Mickey Mantle sat in a drawing room of a train speeding to Washington, D. C. He sat with George Weiss and co-owners Del Webb and Dan Topping. And Mickey Mantle signed a Yankee contract. His salary for the 1951 season was $6,000.

Now there remained only for Mickey to prove himself under actual game conditions. *Only?* Now the pressure was really on Mickey Mantle, for already he was looked upon as an epic hero. Even the Yankee ballplayers stood in awe of his raw talent. But they admired him as a person.

Through all the spring hysteria, Mickey had remained true to himself, essentially a modest, shy, retiring personality. He did have an open personality for his friends. "Even that first year," Phil Rizzuto remembers, "he had kind of a dry humor. When he opened up, there wasn't a funnier guy around."

Mickey, in his Oklahoma twang, told his teammates the joke about these two hunters who go up to their cabin in the mountains. One guy grabs his gun and starts hunting bear while his buddy stays behind and decides to clean up the cabin. The guy who went out looking for a bear sees a big one, drops his gun in fright and makes a beeline for the cabin. Just as he gets to the open door, he falls down and the bear trips over him and lands inside the cabin. "You skin this one," the guy who fell down says to his partner as he gets up and starts running in the opposite direction, "while I go out and get us another one."

The fans themselves had no knowledge of this part of Mickey Mantle, but they were enthusiastic about Mantle the ballplayer. As far as they were concerned, there was Joe DiMaggio and now there was Mickey Mantle. In that spring game against the University of Southern California, Mickey was mobbed for autographs by the students as he attempted to get into the bus carrying the Yankees from the ball field. He began to receive more requests for autographs, more fan mail, than any other Yankee save DiMaggio—and this before he had even officially become a Yankee. People were even sending him poems. One went like this:

> *DiMaggio recognized his*
> *ability for the game*
> *And predicted he'd make*
> *the Hall of Fame.*
> *At 19, talented and very*
> *able,*
> *Mickey's skill is not a*
> *fable.*
> *His arm is strong, his*
> *feet swift;*
> *To watch him play gives*
> *one a lift.*

From Union Station in Washington, D. C., Mickey drove in a taxi to the Shoreham Hotel. He was riding with baseball writer Tom Meany. As the cab passed the illuminated dome of the Capitol, Mickey gazed at it in awe.

"So this is our nation's capitol," he said to Meany.

He was still very much the wide-eyed young American country boy, only now he was on the edge of his biggest adventure in life. That night in his hotel room, awaiting the 1951 season's opener, Mickey thrashed around in bed unable to sleep. What would happen in that game, and in the games to follow? How would he do? Because he didn't know, and couldn't know, he felt as though he were lost in a great forest. But he comforted himself by thinking: You're playing with Rizzuto, DiMaggio, Mize, Reynolds, Lopat, Raschi. You're playing with these guys. You can't be too bad.

CHAPTER SEVEN

A SEASON
OF MIXED EMOTIONS

It rained in Washington on the morning of April 13 and Mickey, looking out his hotel window, was disappointed. Since it was only a one-game series, the traditional baseball opener to permit the President of the United States to throw out the first ball of the season, the Yankees packed and returned to New York.

Now the nineteen-year-old Mickey Mantle would make his major league debut at home, at Yankee Stadium. Yankee Stadium. The home of Babe Ruth, of Lou Gehrig, of Joe DiMaggio. Yankee Stadium. The goal of every baseball-minded young boy: Either to visit the magnificent structure or—if the dream was vivid enough—to play there.

Mantle explains his batting grip to Ted Williams. The Boston Red Sox star, now retired, batted .406 in 1951, and no major league player has since finished a season in the .400s.

Yankee Stadium. For Mickey Mantle, the dream of playing in Yankee Stadium was about to come true.

It was a cool, clear, typically early spring day in New York and Mickey was at the stadium early. He went out early partly to get the feel of "home," but mostly to check manager Casey Stengel's starting lineup. He still found it difficult to believe that he was a part of this team, the world champions of baseball.

There it was, pasted to the dugout wall, the opening day batting order against the Boston Red Sox:

Jackie Jensen	LF
Phil Rizzuto	SS
Mickey Mantle	RF
Joe DiMaggio	CF
Yogi Berra	C
Johnny Mize	1B
Billy Johnson	3B
Jerry Coleman	2B
Vic Raschi	P

Not only was Mickey Mantle the sole rookie in that starting lineup, he was the only Yankee player in history to leap from Class C to a starting lineup on opening day. "Last year he's a shortstop at Joplin," said Casey Stengel before the game. "Today he's in right field in the stadium. More people here watching the kid in one game than watched him the whole last season. I'm praying for him."

Actually, Casey was slightly in error. Before the game, coach Jim Turner caught Mickey gazing wide-eyed at the huge crowd filling the upper tier that envelops the stadium like a horseshoe.

"How many people watched you play in Joplin last year?" Turner asked Mickey.

"I'd say about 55,000 all season," Mickey said.

"Well, take a good look. We got about 45,000 here today, for one game, almost as many people as you saw in Joplin all year."

"No!" exclaimed the rookie.

"Yes," said Turner. "And most of 'em have come to see what you look like."

The people came, they saw, and they were not disappointed.

He came to bat in the last half of the first inning, standing at the plate right-handed against the southpaw slants of Red Sox veteran Bill Wight. He used a modified spread stance of about 24 inches, and he strode about six inches. He gripped his bat at the end, a 36-ounce model. He held his arms away from his body. He wiggled the bat nervously a few times, staring intently at the pitcher. As Wight went into his windup, Mickey cocked his bat. He was ready.

There was no explosion in that first major league contact with major league pitching in the first major league game of his life. Mickey swung hard at a curve ball, but caught it at his fists and broke his bat. Bobby Doerr, the Red Sox second baseman, fielded the ground ball cleanly and threw out Mantle by a half-step. What impressed the spectators that first time at bat, was the way Mickey fled down the base paths.

In the top half of the second inning, Mickey got his first chance in right field. Red Sox first baseman Walt Dropo lifted a routine fly to right field. Joe DiMaggio, gliding over from center, hollered to Mickey, and Mickey made the catch. Later in the game he made two more put-outs.

In his second at bat, Mickey popped to shortstop Vern Stephens. Then, in the sixth inning, Mickey came up with Jackie Jensen on third and Phil Rizzuto on first. Jensen had doubled and Rizzuto bunted beautifully and beat it out.

Mickey looked out at the pitcher. The pitcher looked in at Mickey. He took a deep breath and fired to the plate, a fast ball. Mickey was ready. He smashed a single between short and third—Mickey's first major league base hit, his first major league run batted in.

Later in the same inning, he scored from second base on a single, churning around the bases like an Olympic 220-runner. As he crossed home plate and jogged into the Yankee dugout, he was greeted by the entire Yankee bench. They congratulated him as though he had hit the game-winning homer. "With that blow," columnist Red Smith later wrote, "Mickey was in the lodge."

The Yankees won 5–0 and after the game Mickey was asked how he felt. "All right at bat," he said, "but Joe had to yell at me a lot in the outfield."

Joe DiMaggio shook his head. "It was only because of the large crowd that I had to do so much yelling. The kid was all right."

In his second major league game, Mickey got another hit, knocked in another run and was batting .333. At the end of his first week in the majors, he was batting .320.

But it wasn't all milk and honey. For one thing, Mickey was striking out a lot. For another, when he did strike out, he had that tendency to get down on himself. On April 20 in Washington, Mickey was having his troubles with

Sandy Consuegra, the veteran Senator pitcher. Going into the ninth inning of that game, Mickey was 0 for 4, including two strikeouts. Before he went up to the plate for the fifth time, Casey patted him on the back.

"Don't take it so hard, boy, you'll wear yourself out. You're bound to run into a lot of such days. Heck, Joe DiMaggio hasn't made a hit today. Yogi Berra hasn't hit one out of the infield. These men are great hitters."

Mickey picked his bat from the rack, turned to Stengel and said, "That's all very fine, but it doesn't help me any. I can do better. I should do better."

This time at bat, Mickey did do better. On a two-strike count, he blasted a triple to the far right-field corner and drove in a run.

A couple of days later against the Athletics, Mickey again went hitless in two straight games, though he almost got his first major league homer, a long soaring drive to the left-field bullpen that was finally hauled down by A's outfielder, Elmer Valo.

The next day, when the team moved to Boston, Casey benched Mantle. He explained, "Right field is very tough to cover in Boston what with the sun and wind. I don't want to put any additional pressure on that boy."

Casey realized that Mickey was being subject to tremendous pressure from all sides. On the Yankees' first western trip, he was treated like a conquering hero, not as a scared rookie. As Coach Turner explained, "Everywhere we went there would be photographers waiting for him at the station and interviews and pictures at the hotel before the ball game. It was enough to disturb any young player who is still in the learning class."

At home it was just the same, maybe worse. Every time he went to the corner to mail a letter, he was mobbed. Jack Orr, a columnist for the New York *Compass*, graphically described how it was for Mantle in those days.

"He shares an apartment with Hank Bauer and Johnny Hopp," Orr wrote. "They get up in the morning, eat breakfast and then grab the D train at the 50th Street stop. From that moment, they're after him.

"After the game he has another gauntlet to run. Kids and girls follow him all the way around the stadium as he gets back to the subway. Teenagers plead, 'Please Mickey, please.' Some older women try to get his attention, too. 'He looked at me, honest, he looked at me,' one young woman of twenty-three or so was heard saying the other day.

"All of which naturally has changed the kid who five months ago was making $33.90 a week in the mines. He doesn't trust people as much as he used to. Once he was eager to answer questions. Now he evades them and digs his spikes in the dirt.

"He is disturbed by the mail and the girls and the kids and the subway rides. He has a feeling that he's being pushed around."

And he was, not only by the hero worshipers, but by sharp promoters who hoped to cash in on Mickey's name and fast-spreading reputation. Early that spring a man came to Mickey and offered to become his personal agent, handling endorsements and personal appearances. Mickey said he was interested and the man drew up a contract which guaranteed Mickey $50,000 a year, but the money was to be split 50-50 between player and agent.

Later a legitimate agent, Frank Scott, told Mantle that he would handle Mickey's affairs for 10 percent of his outside income, but no guarantees. Mickey told Scott about the deal he had already been offered.

"If I were you," said Scott, "I would have the Yankee lawyers check that contract."

A couple of weeks later, Scott bumped into Mantle once more. "I've signed the contract," Mickey said.

"Did you take it to the Yankee lawyers?" Scott asked.

"Nope," said Mantle. "I didn't have to. This fellow had a lawyer for me."

It took several years for Mickey, with the Yankees' help, to break that contract. Today, Mickey is handled by Frank Scott and handled fairly and well.

By the end of the month Mickey's batting average was down to .220, and there was talk in the Yankee front office of the necessity of shipping Mickey to the minors for more seasoning.

But the Yankees took Mickey west with them and, for awhile, the anxieties concerning the rookie vanished.

On May 1, at Comiskey Park, the Yankees faced the Chicago White Sox. Batting left-handed against right-hander Randy Gumpert, Mickey blasted a ball deep into the right-field stands, a 450-foot home run, the first of Mickey's major league career.

Four days later in Sportsman's Park, St. Louis, Mickey had a better reason to shine. In the stands watching the Yankees and Browns was Mickey Mantle's mother, his girl friend, Merlyn, and Merlyn's mother. Batting left-handed against Duane Pillette, Mickey caught a change-up and sent it flying over the right-field barrier, another 450-foot home run. After the game, reporters asked Merlyn what she thought of Mickey's hit. "I expected it," she said. "He promised me he'd do it."

Slowly, Mickey began to raise his average. In the first of a three-game series against Detroit, Mickey was the star. For the first three innings, Detroit's Dizzy Trout had pitched hitless baseball. Then in the top of the fourth, lead-off batter Mantle pushed a bunt towards the first-base side of the mound. Trout came off the mound and started fishing for the ball. By the time he found it, Mickey was already on first base. Mickey went on to score the first Yankee run and the Yankees blasted the game open, winning 11–6. Mickey had three hits for the day.

The next day Mickey displayed his awesome speed, running from first to third on a sacrifice bunt. A few days later against Cleveland, Mickey rifled a single over second base. Indians' outfielder Larry Doby came in to field it and before he knew what was happening, Mickey had cut on a dime and was into second base.

"You ain't seen nothing yet," said Casey Stengel. "This kid doesn't run—he flies. He's positively the fastest guy on the bases I've ever seen and he seems to have the instinct to go with it. They don't throw him out. Not often, they don't."

After the first five weeks of the season, Mickey was back up over .300 and leading the team in runs batted in. The Yankees were in first place and Stengel was wonderfully enthusiastic about Mickey. "He's hitting in all those runs leading off or batting second. He won't always bat way up there, but I don't want him coming up too often with the bases filled and striking out because he's over anxious until he's been around for awhile longer."

As late as May 12, certain Yankee brass were in favor of

sending Mickey out. But he continued to hit, and to learn in the outfield, and he managed to survive the May 15 cut-down date. He was thousands of miles from being a finished ballplayer, but already he was an exciting one.

In Philadelphia one day, Mickey singled to left. Then he streaked from first to third on a single to left, beating Gus Zernial's throw. Only the umpire said Mickey had missed second base. "I don't know about that," Casey said later. "But I can easily see why the umpires thought he did. He got from first to third so fast that they must've thought he ran across the pitcher's box."

Meanwhile, Yankee coaches worked hard with Mantle. They ordered him on the field at 11 each morning at home to take special lessons on bunting. "He hits so hard when he swings now," Stengel said, "that no infielder who has any regard for his teeth can play in for a bunt. And if they play back, he'll be crossing first base just about the time they'll be picking up one of his bunts."

In the field, Tommy Henrich continued to work with Mickey. The youngster found it hard to learn two particular aspects of the outfield—line drives hit directly at him, and where to throw the ball. "When I went out there at first," he recalled, "I thought I'd choke. I was so scared my arms almost tied up on me when I reached for the ball. But what bothers me most is getting the ball where it has to go."

One day against Cleveland, Mickey demonstrated his confusion. With Dale Mitchell on second base, Larry Doby on first, a single was hit to right. Mickey picked up the ball quickly and threw into third, allowing Mitchell to score. He was disgusted with himself.

"I gave up a run," he blazed. "They're not using me to give up runs."

But Henrich made Mickey feel better about the play. "There just isn't one way to make that play," Tommy said. "It could be you did it right, but if you didn't, that won't be the worst mistake you'll ever make. Fellows in the league for ten years still throw to the wrong bases. There's many a throw I wish I could have called back."

As May wore on, Mickey's average began to sag again. Pitchers started throwing him hard and tight, in on the fists, and his hands and wrists were discolored and jarred by the impact of the ball against the thin end of his bat. He struck out a lot and got down on himself and it didn't help when he muffed a few easy flies. Sometimes he had to play a sun field and he was slow to flick down the sunglasses and Stengel occasionally went into an angry monologue on Mickey's play.

"He can run faster than any other outfielder in the business," Casey would moan, "but one never would know that from watching him out there." And he would exhort Mickey, "Put on a show, boy. Run hard for the ball. Haul off. Throw a foot high into the air when you heave the ball. Don't be afraid to throw."

At this time Stengel also began to feel, based on statistics, that Mickey might be a more capable batter left-handed. He even suggested to reporters that "the boy"—he always called him the boy—should abandon switch-hitting. If Mickey heard Stengel, he paid no attention. He went about his job quietly and stubbornly. His father had taught him to be a switch-hitter, and a switch-hitter he would remain.

On May 30, 1951, Mickey had one of the most frustrating days of his life. In the first game of a double-header with the Red Sox, batting right-handed against southpaw Chuck Stobbs, he struck out three straight times. Then his first two times up in the second game he struck out twice more. Five consecutive strikeouts and Mickey felt as if the world had fallen in on him. In the dugout, he began to cry. "Put somebody in there who can hit," he told Stengel. "I can't."

Stengel consoled Mickey as best he could, then announced that he would play the youngster only against right-handers, so that he would bat only left-handed. With a southpaw opposing the Yankees, Jackie Jensen played right field.

For awhile, Mickey's hitting picked up. In the middle of June he had a seven-game hitting streak, which put him back near .300. On June 20 in two games against the White Sox, he drove in four runs, which gave him a runs-batted-in total of 42, tops on the Yankees. He also hit his fourth home run.

But he couldn't maintain this level. He stopped batting in runs. He stopped hitting. By July 15 he was down to .260. He had hit seven home runs, nine doubles, five triples, and 45 runs batted in. But in 69 games he had struck out 52 times. That day the worried boy was called into the Yankee front office.

Weiss and Stengel were there and as gently as possible, they informed Mantle that they were shipping him out on option to Kansas City, subject to 24-hour recall. "We need pitching help right now," they told Mickey. "But we'll try to bring you up later this season."

Mickey left that conference with tears in his eyes.

The Yankees called up Art Schallock, a twenty-six-year-old left-hander, in exchange for Mantle. Casey, whose will had been heeded all season when Weiss had wanted to send Mantle down, explained his feelings later to newsmen.

"The boy is good and make no mistake about that. He came up as a shortstop, but we converted him into a right fielder and overnight he showed me he could do everything—run, field, throw and hit a long ball. They don't come any faster.

"However," Casey went on, "he had one weakness. He struck out too often. But I'm certain he'll overcome that and he'll be back."

The Yankees backed up their convictions about Mantle by ordering Kansas City to play Mickey in center field. They were convinced that Mantle would be Joe Di-Maggio's replacement.

As for Mickey himself, he masked his disappointment as bravely as he could. "It's all right with me," he said. "I'd rather play every day in the minors than sit on the Yankee bench. Nobody has to tell me that I've got plenty to learn about outfielding and hitting."

He left the Yankees in Detroit and joined Kansas City in Milwaukee. In his first time at bat for Kansas City, Mickey beat out a bunt. His next 19 times at bat, he was unable to get a base hit.

He returned with the club in Kansas City in a grave personal crisis, "the worst time of my life," he later admitted. But help was coming for Mickey.

Mutt Mantle had read in the papers about Mickey's

helplessness, and he told his wife, "I'm going to take a couple of days off and see what's what with Mickey."

Mutt was confronted with a boy who was completely down on himself. Mickey blurted to his father, "I'm just not cut out for baseball. Maybe I ought to quit."

Mutt looked his boy squarely in the eye. "If that's all the guts you got," he said, "pack up and come home with me now and be a miner."

Mickey was shocked, but his father would not let up. He said sternly to Mickey, "You can't have it easy all your life. Baseball is no different from any other job. Things get tough once in a while and you must learn how to take it. And the sooner, the better."

"I'm sorry, Dad," Mickey said. Mutt Mantle smiled and told his son he would come to Kansas City—which was 150 miles from Commerce—as often as possible.

The next day Mickey started hitting. One game late in July against Columbus, he hit two home runs, a triple, a double and a bunt single. By August 20, Mickey had appeared in 40 games for Kansas City. His batting average was .361; he had made 60 hits, 11 home runs and driven in 50 runs. The Yankees, in a desperate pennant struggle with the Cleveland Indians, called Mickey back.

Mickey took the promotion calmly. "I think the time I spent with the Blues at Kansas City helped a lot," he said, "but," he added warily, "maybe they're just calling me back to give me a few more pointers."

But before he could rejoin the Yankees, Mickey received another call. The Army wanted to examine Mickey once more. He flew to Fort Sill, Oklahoma, where *six* physicians, including the Fourth Army's orthopedic specialist, put him under a microscopic examination. An Army spokesman explained, "He's receiving an unusually thorough examination so there will be no doubt as to his condition, and whether he is eligible to serve."

Then came the news. All six doctors verified that Mickey was still suffering from osteomyelitis. They all agreed that Mickey was "unacceptable by present Army standards."

But he was most acceptable to the Yankees. The day after he rejoined the club, Mickey was back in the starting lineup. And he hit a two-run home run off Mike Garcia as the Yankees whipped Cleveland, 7–3. A week later, in St. Louis, with his family watching, Mickey hit a home run and a single and drove in four runs.

One weekend in August at Yankee Stadium, he showed hometown fans how he had improved. Going into the last of the seventh, the Yanks' Ed Lopat and the Washington Senators' Bob Porterfield were locked in a scoreless pitching duel. Then the Yankees started on Porterfield, putting two men on base, with Mickey coming to bat.

Mantle stood at the plate, left-handed, watching the canny Porterfield. As Porterfield pumped, Mickey raised his bat. As Porterfield delivered, Mickey braced. As the ball came screaming towards the plate, Mickey swung. And away it went, a tremendous, ripping line drive that landed deep in the right-field bleachers 450 feet from home plate. It was one of the longest home runs seen at Yankee Stadium all year. Three runs crossed the plate and the Yankees went on to win, 4–0.

The next day, the Yankees met the Senators in a doubleheader. In the first game, as the Yankees were winning

7–5, Mickey hit another home run. In the second game, limited to five and a half innings because of darkness, the Yankees won 2–0 and Mickey scored one of the two runs. The double victory put the Yankees in first place by .004 in the percentages.

Since his return from Kansas City, Mickey was delivering in the clutch. He still wasn't hitting for any great average, but he was producing when runs were needed.

How well he was producing is best illustrated by a crucial three-game series in Fenway Park, Boston, the final week of the season. The Yankees led Cleveland only by a game and a half, all in the win column. Had they blown this series, the Indians might have passed the Yankees. But Mickey drove the last spike in the Cleveland coffin. In those last three games he hit a homer, two triples, two doubles. He batted in six runs. And in the series opener, with the Yankees leading 1–0 in the sixth inning, Mickey made a superb throw to nab Dom DiMaggio at first base after Dom had made the wide turn rounding the bag.

On September 28, the Yankees clinched another pennant, and Mickey Mantle had made his contributions. He was no rookie standout—Willie Mays was the star rookie in the National League, Minnie Minoso and teammate Gil McDougald in the American. But Mickey was now very much a major-leaguer.

The final figures showed that Mickey had played in 96 games, had batted 341 times for a .267 average: 91 singles, 11 doubles, 5 triples, 13 home runs and 65 runs batted in. In the 37 games after leaving Kansas City, his average was .283.

And so to the World Series.

It was the miracle New York Giants, riding in by virtue of Bobby Thomson's miracle home run in the third play-off game against the Brooklyn Dodgers. Most everybody favored the Yankees in the World Series. About the only thing the New York writers were guessing about was whether Mickey would crack the starting lineup.

Mickey was guessing too, but the night before the opening of the World Series, he found his name on top of the Yankee batting order. He would lead off and play right field.

"I didn't believe it," Mickey said at the time. "I thought Stengel would go with the same lineup that clinched the pennant against the Red Sox."

The day of the game, Mickey Mantle, by his own admission, felt ten times tighter than when he had played his first big league game. He was caught up in the fever of World Series excitement that had hit New York hard, especially since it was a subway World Series. And Mickey's family was coming in. Mickey's dad was not feeling too well, he was having back trouble, but he drove all the way from Commerce with an uncle and three other men.

Early on the morning of the first game, Mickey took his dad and uncle on a sightseeing tour of the city.

He got to the stadium at 10:30, hit well in batting practice, but hit nothing in the first game. In fact no one hit well for the Yankees as they went down to the Giants, 5–1.

The next day Larry Jansen was the pitcher and Mickey was in right field again. Leading off in the bottom of the first, he dragged a bunt single, his first World Series hit. In the third inning he struck out.

Casey Stengel (37) introduces Mantle to President Eisenhower before the opening game of the 1956 World Series. Other Yanks line up to meet the President.

In the top of the fifth, Willie Mays came to bat for the Giants. Mantle was shaded toward right center, figuring Willie to pull. Willie caught hold of the ball, a high fly that headed toward right center, between Mantle and Joe DiMaggio. Mickey drifted towards the ball, heard DiMaggio call for it. At that instant, Mickey felt something pop in his knee. Suddenly, he fell in a heap.

DiMaggio made the catch and then bent down over Mantle. "What's the matter, kid?" he asked. Mickey was too frightened to answer.

They carried him off the field on a stretcher to the clubhouse where Dr. Sidney Gaynor, the Yankee physician, packed the knee in ice and put a stiff elastic bandage around it.

Newsmen crowded in on Mantle after the game, which the Yankees had won, 3–1. By now Mickey had regained some of his composure.

"What happened?" they asked. Everyone thought that Mantle had tripped over a sprinkler hole. There is a waterage outlet in that right-center area, covered by a wooden trapdoor that would give a little if stepped on.

"I may have run over that hole," Mickey said, "but I just don't know. All I know is that one second I was running and the next second the knee was giving out. I fell and stayed on the ground. I was really scared. I was thinking about a broken leg."

Mutt Mantle hurried to the Yankee clubhouse, deeply concerned about his son. He drove in a taxi with Mickey to Lenox Hill Hospital. As Mutt tried to help Mickey out of the cab, the father suddenly collapsed to the street.

And so it was that Mickey Mantle watched the rest of

the World Series on television, watched as the Yankees swept the rest of the games, watched with his leg propped up—the diagnosis, a torn ligament on the inner side of the right leg—watched with his father in the bed next to him. Mutt Mantle was ill, gravely ill with cancer.

Mickey's first year in the majors was over, and in many ways, he was glad it was behind him.

CHAPTER EIGHT

FOUND: A CENTER FIELDER

His knee still feeling very weak, Mickey was discharged from the hospital in New York and, on crutches, limped back to Commerce, Oklahoma, to rest and try to build up the strength in his knee. The Mayo Clinic gave him weights to lift with his right leg, in order to exercise and strengthen his knee. Mickey worked with them for two weeks then, feeling his knee was stronger, quit. He started kicking a football around. It was a mistake.

For quite awhile, too, he wore a brace, plus a special weighted boot. He and a hometown friend spent much of the winter tramping through the woods in search of quail and rabbit. Not only was Mickey doing something he loved, but hunting, at least, was also effective therapy for his leg.

On December 11, 1951, an announcement that would have an important bearing on Mantle's future was made in New York. After thirteen active seasons as a Yankee, thirteen seasons in which the Yankees won ten pennants and nine world championships, Joe DiMaggio formally called it quits. Immediately, manager Casey Stengel told the press that he expected Mantle to fill DiMaggio's old position.

Mickey was flattered by Stengel's vote of confidence. "It will be impossible for anyone to take Joe's place, he's so great," said Mickey. "But they can count on me doing the best I can. I promise that much."

But Mickey also knew he would have to fight for the center field job. The Yankees had another good-looking youngster, Jackie Jensen, and he was an accomplished outfielder and an excellent hitting prospect. There was also Gene Woodling, Hank Bauer and Bob Cerv. Mantle had no illusions about how easy it would be to step into the shoes of the Yankee Clipper.

On December 23, 1951, Mickey and Merlyn Louise Johnson were married. And it was as a family man that Mickey reported to the Yankees at their new spring training base in St. Petersburg, Florida.

This time it was far different than a year ago, when Mantle, an unheralded rookie, had flashed so stunningly. Now he was a one-year veteran and everyone knew what he could do—at least knew his potential. The question was could he live up to his potential? It was a question that would haunt Mickey Mantle throughout his baseball career.

He was handicapped from the beginning in the spring of 1952. His knee simply had not fully healed and Mickey was unable to go at full speed. He didn't break into the starting lineup until March 18, two weeks after the start of the exhibition season. And then it was in right field. He stayed in right field until April 5, then was tried in center field. Before the Yankees' opening game of the season against the Philadelphia Athletics, the big guessing contest among the fans was who would start in center field for the Yankees—Jackie Jensen or Mickey Mantle?

Jensen won. In that opening game, Jackie played center, but Mickey was in the starting lineup in right field. He got two singles and a double, drove in two runs and had four put-outs. But through those early games he stayed in right field, as Jensen and Cerv alternated in center.

Mickey was not happy. He began to make the same mistakes that he had made as a rookie. He was striking out a lot, and he was having troubles in the outfield. In one early season game, a ball was looped between right and center field. Both Jensen and Mantle converged on it. Jackie hollered for Mickey to take it. The ball bounced off Mantle's glove and smacked him in the right temple. "I was so ashamed," Mickey remembered later, "I wanted to die right there."

Casey Stengel wasn't at all satisfied with what was going on. While he was maneuvering his outfield like a frantic chess master, the Yankees were floundering. He and general manager George Weiss decided to make a drastic change. On May 3 Jackie Jensen, the Yankees' opening day center fielder, was traded to Washington—Jensen, pitcher Frank Shea and utility infielder Archie Wilson, for another center fielder, Irv Noren.

Now Noren took a shot at center field.

On May 6, Mickey received a grievous blow. His father, the man who had made him a ballplayer, was dead of cancer. Mickey was grief-stricken. "He was a real good guy," Mickey said. "I only hope I can be as good as he wanted me to be."

Mickey went home to Commerce for the funeral and, fighting back his tears, he began to realize the full significance of his father's death. Now he was the man of the family. Now it was up to him to support his dad's family as well as his own. "Baseball had been just a game before Dad died," Mickey said later. "After his death, it became a profession. I had to make it."

Mickey rejoined the Yankees with his .260 batting average and, for awhile, played right field. In a game against Cleveland on May 13, Mickey was not in the starting lineup. But in the fifth inning, on a brainstorm of Casey's, he was inserted into third base, for Bobby Brown. Mickey made two hits in that game, but he also made two errors. Finally, on May 20, Mickey Mantle's name was inserted in the lineup in center field.

Batting third against the Chicago White Sox, and batting left-handed against Ken Holcombe, Mickey singled twice. Then, when left-hander Chuck Stobbs came in to relieve Holcombe, Mantle turned around at the plate and singled twice more. His average jumped to .315 and the Yankees had found themselves a center fielder.

For the rest of that 1952 season, Mickey, along with pitcher Allie Reynolds, was one of the two most valuable men on the team. Mickey's improvement was rapid and impressive.

On June 3 against Billy Pierce of the Chicago White Sox, Mickey had another four-hit day. He also scored the Yankees' winning run in the 13th inning.

Two weeks later at Detroit, Mickey hit a huge home run against Billy Hoeft. The ball landed in the upper deck of the left-center field bleachers at Briggs Stadium, a 450-foot clout and the longest home run he had yet hit as a right-hander.

He had one of his biggest days on July 13. For the first time, Mickey hit a home run left-handed and right-handed the same day. It was a doubleheader and in the first game Mickey hit a home run left-handed into the right-field stands at Yankee Stadium. Against veteran southpaw Hal Newhouser in the second game, Mickey hit a right-handed homer into the left-field stands.

One of his biggest days came late in July against the White Sox. The Yankees had lost six out of seven games and their pennant lead was in jeopardy. It looked like seven out of eight as Billy Pierce had the Yankees blanked, 7–0. In the top of the seventh, Mickey doubled in a run and later scored himself, and the margin was cut to 7–3.

It was still 7–3 going into the top of the ninth. Gil McDougald, the first batter, flied out. Gene Woodling singled. Yogi Berra walked. Johnny Mize, pinch-hitting, singled Woodling home. Kal Segrist, another pinch-hitter, grounded to third and Allie Reynolds, running for Mize, went to second. Jim Brideweser then grounded to third but White Sox third baseman Hector Rodriguez bobbled the ball and Berra scored.

The score was now 7–5, two outs, and Chicago brought in a new pitcher, Chuck Stobbs. Stobbs walked Joe Collins, filling the bases. Irv Noren also walked, forcing home the Yankees' sixth run.

The score was 7–6, two men out, the bases loaded and Mickey Mantle up right-handed. And Mickey delivered. He smashed the first pitch into the lower left-field stands, clearing the bases and wrapping up a 10–7 Yankee victory. It was Mickey's second grand-slam home run in four days.

That was one of Mickey's best clutch performances of the year, but there were others as the Yankees drove down the stretch.

Against the Red Sox before 48,797 fans at the stadium, the biggest home crowd of the year, Mickey shone again. His first two times up, Mickey reached base safely, both on errors by Ted Lepcio, who apparently was so shaken by Mickey's speed that he failed to handle Mantle ground balls. In the bottom of the sixth with the Red Sox leading 2–1, Yogi Berra tripled and Mickey flied deep to center for the sacrifice that scored Yogi with the tying run.

In the eighth inning, Mickey singled to right. Bobby Brown doubled to right and Mickey raced all the way home with the winning run.

After the game, old Casey was beaming. "Sure, I think Mantle is the most improved player in the league. Why shouldn't I? Ever since we put the kid in center regularly, we've been winning regularly, haven't we?"

Lou Boudreau, the Red Sox manager, felt essentially the same. "Without him," Lou said, "they would have been just another team this year. With him, they're the leaders. There's no question in my mind he's going to be one of the greatest."

Mickey turned it on down the stretch. On September

21, the Yankees went into Cleveland leading the Indians by only a game and a half. With 73,000 fans watching, Mickey made believers out of them all. He doubled and homered as the Yankees beat tough Mike Garcia.

On September 24, he tormented the Red Sox again, this time at Boston. In the first game of a doubleheader, Mickey doubled in the first Yankee run. It was a tie game going into the tenth, but Mickey's tenth inning triple gave the Yankees a 3–2 victory. In the second game, won by the Yankees 8–6, Mickey singled, tripled and homered and drove in four runs.

Two days later in Philadelphia, the Yankees clinched the pennant, 5–2 and Mantle helped celebrate with a home run.

Mickey had done more than his share in the drive for the pennant. Over the full 1952 season he had ripped 37 doubles, 7 triples and 23 home runs, 12 right-handed, 11 left-handed. He had driven in 87 runs and his .311 batting average was third best in the league. The only demerits against him were his 111 strikeouts, a new Yankee record, and his 14 errors, high for an American League outfielder that year.

These flaws of course bothered Mickey. "In the field," he said, "line drives straight at me are still trouble. I can't tell if a ball's hit real good or if it's going to drop in front of me. At bat I'm weak on the fast ball high inside. Curves on the outside give me trouble. I'm getting to bunt better, but I still have a tendency to bunt up at the ball and pop it up. I still got to learn not to swing at bad balls. I certainly swung at too many last year."

But a fellow American Leaguer, Larry Doby of the

Indians, who also struck out 111 times, was in full sympathy with Mantle. "Anybody swings as hard as Mantle or
me is going to strike out a lot. They might tell him, 'Take
it easy on the swing and you'll hit .400.' But how can you
tell a boy that? It's natural for him to swing hard and he
always will."

Probably the toughest pitcher for Mickey to handle was
bespectacled Walt Masterson of the Senators. In one game,
Masterson struck out Mantle four times in a row. But
Masterson was quick to excuse this indiscretion.

"I don't own him," Walt said at the time. "I get him
out on curves. One after the other. I remember whipping
over five straight strikes on curves. Then I tried to cross
him up with a fast ball and he pulled it hard down the
right-field line, but foul. So I came in with the curve
again and got him again. Maybe next year, it will be
different. Other pitchers throw him curves and he belts
'em. Maybe that's the way Mickey will treat me next time.
Who can tell? With his power he can go a long, long way.
Nobody will ever catch me bragging about how I got
Mickey out."

The fact remains that Mickey, through his brilliant play
from June on, was the most improved player in the game,
and the best second-year performer for 1952. The man
who best put this improvement into words was a victim,
Marty Marion, then manager of the St. Louis Browns.

"He was a much bigger problem for our pitchers in
August than he was in April," Marion pointed out. "In
fact, I'd say he was a hundred percent improved at the
season's end this year than he was at the start. For a fellow
who broke into baseball as a shortstop, Mantle certainly

has learned a great deal about playing the outfield in the short time he has been doing it. Can you remember the last time you saw him throw to the wrong base? I can't.

"There's no sure way of getting him out when he comes to the plate. We tried everything. Sure, we got him out occasionally. But the same pitch we fooled him on one time, he walloped for extra bases the next time up. That's the tipoff on an outstanding hitter."

It remained then only for the World Series.

This time Mickey was a lot looser than he had been for the World Series of 1951. After all, he was a two-year veteran of major league ball, respected by most of his elders, especially American League pitchers. The National League champion Brooklyn Dodgers could also be expected to treat Mickey respectfully.

But Mickey himself was not in a respectful mood.

In the first game Joe Black, a rookie from Morgan State College, who had been a one-man pitching staff for the Dodgers most of the year, started against Allie Reynolds. The Dodgers hit three home runs—Jackie Robinson, Pee Wee Reese and Duke Snider—and the only Yankee to make more than one hit was Mickey Mantle. He collected two singles. The Dodgers won, 4–2.

It was a different story the next day. Vic Raschi, the Springfield Rifle, took the mound for the Yankees. His opponent was Carl Erskine. The Dodgers scored a run in the third to take the lead. But the Yankees scored one in the fourth, one in the fifth and five big ones in the sixth, climaxed by a three-run homer by Billy Martin. Mickey Mantle? He had another good day—three for five, a double and two sharp singles.

The third game was played in Yankee Stadium, Preacher Roe opposing Eddie Lopat. And it was the Dodgers' turn again. Roe gave up only six hits in a 5–2 Dodger victory, including a home run by Yogi Berra and a pinch-homer by Johnny Mize. Mickey Mantle went scoreless, the only time of the seven games that he would be blanked. But he performed a feat in the field that even today is remembered by baseball veterans. It was accurately described in *Sport* magazine some years ago by baseball columnist Milton Gross.

"In the eighth inning, Jackie Robinson slashed a single to center. As Robinson made a sharp swerve around first base, Mickey fielded the ball on one hop and then was faced with a choice that every National League outfielder has had to make. He could throw to second, forcing Robinson to retreat to first base, or hold his throw until Jackie had committed himself irrevocably when it would be Mantle's arm against Jackie's speed, daring and know-how on the bases. When it is you against Robinson, it is no simple decision to make.

"Mantle elected to hold his throw. Whether it was a deliberate or instinctive decision, none can say, but Mantle watched Robinson and Jackie, watching the fielder, came as much as twenty-five feet toward second. He slowed down, pretending to go back and Mickey, meanwhile, came in several steps with the ball before cocking his arm as if to throw to first base.

"With that motion, Jackie went into high gear for second, yet Mantle still held his throw. Suddenly, it seemed Jackie sensed he could not make the base. The Dodger stopped, stumbled, got to his feet again and then scrambled back to first.

"It was a war of nerves on the bases, Robinson drawing on his years of experience and Mantle drawing from some inexplicable well of wisdom that seemed to be his despite his youth, and it was a war Robinson lost."

Gross later pointed out the shrewd reaction to the dramatic play by Branch Rickey, the discoverer of Jackie Robinson. Rickey, at the game, turned to his companion and said, "Maturity is something that cannot be measured in years. That young man's arms and legs and eyes and wind are young, but his head is old. To me it is the final proof of the boy. Mantle has the chance to make us forget every ballplayer we ever saw."

Meanwhile, though, the Yankees were down two games to one in the Series and they were engaged in a war. Allie Reynolds put the war on even footing again when he dueled with Joe Black and shut out the Dodgers, 2–0. Johnny Mize's home run helped decide the game, and Mickey Mantle chipped in with a triple and scored the other Yankee run.

The fifth game in the stadium, before a crowd of 70,536, was a tense, brilliant, 11-inning affair. Despite another Johnny Mize homer, Carl Erskine managed to hold the Yankees, 6–5. Mickey Mantle got one hit for the day.

In every one of those first five games, Mantle had contributed something. But now he got down to business. For five innings of the sixth game, a make-or-break game for the Yankees, it was a scoreless battle between Billy Loes and Vic Raschi. In the last of the sixth, Duke Snider homered to give the Dodgers a one-run lead. But in the top of the seventh, Yogi Berra homered, Gene Woodling singled, advanced to second and scored when Vic Raschi singled off pitcher Loes' leg.

With the score a slim 2–1 in the top of the eighth, Mickey came up to the plate. He wasted no time. He blasted a 400-foot home run off Loes. It was the clinching run for the Yankees because Snider hit another home run in the last of the eighth for the Dodgers.

Now it was down to the seventh game, and no place to hide. It was Joe Black vs. Ed Lopat and for three innings nobody could score. In the fourth both teams scored a run. In the fifth, both teams scored again. Then, in the top of the sixth, Mickey came up left-handed against Black. He hit a Black fast ball and it went all the way. The Yankees led, 3–2.

An inning later, batting right-handed, Mickey lined a Preacher Roe curve ball into left field for a single that drove in the fourth run. Those two runs made the difference—the difference in the game, and the difference in the Series between two equally matched teams. The Yankees were world champions again, and twenty-year-old Mickey Mantle was the hero.

Afterward in the somber Dodger dressing room, Jackie Robinson sat on a trunk propped against the wall. There were tears in his eyes and disbelief in his voice when he spoke of Mickey Mantle.

"I didn't think he could do it," Jackie said. "He made 'em forget Joe DiMaggio."

In the seven-game Series, Mantle had batted .345. He made ten hits, including two homers, a triple and a double. He scored five runs. He batted in three big runs. He also handled 16 outfield chances perfectly.

Was it any wonder then that the folks in Commerce, Oklahoma, should prepare a celebration for the hometown hero? When Mickey returned to Commerce, he returned in style. The schoolchildren were given the day off. An afternoon football game between Northeastern Oklahoma A & M and Eastern Oklahoma A & M was moved to Commerce from Miami just for the occasion. Along the seven long blocks of Commerce's main street, the street lights were decked with bunting. There were bands from Miami, Picher, Quapao, Fairland, Chelsea, Grover, Commerce—sixteen in all.

An estimated crowd of 7,500—three times the population of Commerce—lined the streets to greet Mickey. Uniformed police from Joplin, Baxter Springs, Galena and Miami as well as units of the highway patrol from Kansas, Missouri and Oklahoma added to the color. The governor's representative made Mickey an honorary colonel and a caravan of cars and bands and drill units marched past the pool hall, the Black Hat Café, the town hall, Otis Chandler's drugstore and other Commerce landmarks. Mickey's three brothers, sister and mother rode in one car. Mickey rode in another with his wife Merlyn. He couldn't help reading the signs in the store windows, and he couldn't help blushing. One read, "Our Mickey of the New York Yankees is the most sensational rookie of all time. . . ." Another said: "All Commerce is proud of Mickey Mantle. A country boy who made good in the big city."

Mickey said he "felt silly about the whole thing. There I was sitting with Merlyn in the back of the big open Cadillac riding up the street and all those people hollering it up for me and I didn't even know what to say or do. What's so special about me?"

There was something very special about the modest Mr. Mantle and that night at a banquet for Mickey, various speakers tried to put it in words. Tom Greenwade, the scout who discovered Mickey, spoke. So did Mickey's teammate and fellow Oklahoman Allie Reynolds, and so did the mayor. When it came time for Mickey to get up, what could he say? He rose, smiled, looked at the crowd and drawled, "Thanks to everybody."

And that's all they expected him to say.

CHAPTER NINE

GOOD, NOT GREAT

The young Mickey Mantle who celebrated his twenty-first birthday on October 21, 1952, at home with his wife, her parents, and his kid brothers and sisters looking in, was not the Mickey Mantle the world knows today. He was still essentially the hometown boy, shy and distrustful of the world outside, uncertain of his own talents and whether they would develop in the extravagant manner predicted by the experts. Despite a fine baseball season in 1952, capped by a brilliant World Series, Mickey Mantle was still far from at peace with himself.

There were a lot of things that bothered him. For one, he still felt uncomfortable talking to strangers. He was especially harassed by feature writers and reporters all demanding his time, all asking the same questions. Once he confided to a teammate, "I wish they'd leave me alone."

"When they start leaving you alone, kid," said the teammate, "you'll know that you don't count anymore."

This shyness didn't apply to his teammates. Mickey was a different person with them and they all liked him. They appreciated his growing value to the ball club. They also liked him for himself, for his wry sense of humor and his boyish enthusiasms.

Mickey became especially friendly with two Yankee regulars, Whitey Ford and Billy Martin. They buddied around together on the road (Mickey and Martin roomed together)—going to movies together, eating in restauarants together, playing practical jokes on each other, and on some of the other players. Phil Rizzuto says that when Mickey loosened up there wasn't a funnier guy around.

"I remember one spring we were barnstorming through Texas," Rizzuto said. "Coming back from the ball park to the hotel, Mickey and Billy Martin disappeared. They showed up later wearing ten-gallon hats with bullet holes in them. 'We had a gun duel,' Mickey said straight-faced.

"In infield practice they used to make believe they were killing each other violently. Mantle would reach behind his shoulder and pull out an imaginary arrow and wing Martin. Billy always used to retaliate by throwing hand grenades.

"I used to be a butt of a lot of their practical jokes, too. They knew how I hated bugs and lizards and spiders and creatures like that, and they were always stuffing my locker with them. Once, Mickey and Whitey Ford hung a dead mouse over the steering wheel of my car. I jumped when

I saw that, I tell you. And there was one spring when I drove south in a little British car. After practice one day I got into the car, started it—and—boom. There was an explosion and smoke came belching out from under the hood, and I was out the door, running for dear life. Mantle had attached a giant firecracker to the starter."

It was all in good fun and Mickey and his teammates appreciated each other. But it was a different story between Mickey and his public. Starting in his rookie year, Mickey began to be booed by fans, both at Yankee Stadium and on the road. In 1952, when he was having a good year, the boos continued much shriller. Even the veteran manager, Casey Stengel, couldn't understand what was going on.

"At one point last summer," Casey said referring to 1952, "they tried to boo my kid right outta town. Right here at Yankee Stadium, where I never thought I'd ever see it, they tried to boo him back to the bench. He doesn't have to make a bad peg or anything to get booed. He can do more things better than anybody else, but they give it to him, anyway. It's not right."

Mickey himself was unable to fathom the attitude of the baseball public. "I've tried to figure it out," Mickey said, "but I don't understand it. I try as hard as I can and do the best I can but sometimes it doesn't seem to be enough. It just seems that the fans want to boo and nothing will stop them.

"I'm not complaining," he said. "Ballplayers have no right to complain about the fans booing. But it sure makes me feel better when they cheer."

What were the reasons for the boos that began swelling around Mickey's head in 1951, that increased in volume in

1952 and 1953 and on through the years? There were three.

One: Mickey had succeeded Joe DiMaggio, the greatest Yankee hero since Babe Ruth. The fans had grown to love Joe, especially in his declining years with the Yankees. And they asked each other, "Who is this young squirt trying to fill the shoes of our Joe?" It was an unfair attitude to take because Mickey never asked to be Joe DiMaggio and never claimed he was. Yet the comparison was drawn.

Two: Mickey's status in the military draft. If he had been anyone but Mickey Mantle, he would have been examined once, been declared 4–F and that would have been the end of it. But with a war on in Korea, Mickey Mantle came to be some sort of a symbol, an unfair symbol, of the physically able young man shirking his duty.

In November of 1952, while Mickey was working for Harold Youngman, a contractor in Baxter Springs, Missouri, he was called for the fourth time by his draft board. Again he was turned down. This time it wasn't only the osteomyelitis, but also a chronic defect in his right knee that was aggravated by the 1951 World Series accident.

And still, Mickey's draft board got letters of complaint from people who wanted to know why Mickey could play baseball but not serve in the Army.

Three: The tape measure. Since Joe DiMaggio's retirement, the Yankees needed another gate attraction. So they built up Mantle, and one way they pushed the buildup was through a device called the tape measure. In April of 1953, the first tape measure was dragged out to measure the distance of a Mickey Mantle home run.

The season started innocently enough for Mickey. In

fact, it started happily. On April 12, an eig... ounce boy was born to Mickey and Merlyn. H... Mickey Elven Mantle.

Five days later, Mickey gave his first born a specia...

There were 4,206 paid customers at Griffith Stadium... Washington, D. C., to see the Yankees play the Senators. A lot of them were curious to see this fellow Mantle who, eight days earlier, had been hailed for hitting a monster home run in Pittsburgh. That ball was driven onto the right-field roof of Forbes Field. Mickey became only the third man in history to hit a ball that far in Pittsburgh.

Now it came to the fifth inning in Washington, the Yankees ahead, 2–1. Yogi Berra on first. Chuck Stobbs, Washington southpaw, was on the mound. Mantle came up to the plate right-handed. The first ball came in tight, Mickey let it go by. Ball one.

A raw wind bit into Stobbs' face as he got ready to throw the next pitch. He picked up the rosin bag, dropped it, then looked to his catcher for the sign. Mickey waited patiently, staring out at the pitcher, hefting the bat around in his hands, pawing at the plate with his right foot, digging in, and waiting.

Finally, Stobbs stepped on the rubber, took a look at first base, then drew back and fired to the plate. The ball came in thigh-high, over the middle of the plate.

Mickey whipped his arms around in a hissing, upper-cutting arc, throwing all his 185 pounds behind the swing. And he connected. The ball flew off the bat, flew high over the bleacher front wall, 391 feet from home plate; over the bleacher back wall, 66 feet farther back and 55 feet high; caromed over a football scoreboard converted to a beer ad for the baseball season, 50 feet farther back

on a rooftop outside the
...l on 5th Street.

...nkees' publicity director,
...out of the park. On 5th
...old boy named Donald
...away pointed to where he
...e the tape measure. After
...as officially measured at—
...inging right-handed, had
...me run ever hit in a major
league park. ...don't care ...far it went," said Stengel.
"It was the longest ball I ever saw."

Patterson patted Dunaway on the back, gave him $10 and three new baseballs for this historic ball. The ball was taken back to New York and exhibited in the lobby at Yankee Stadium (where it was stolen and then returned by some boys), then shipped to Cooperstown, New York, home of the Hall of Fame, where it resides today. Patterson, commenting later to reporters about the condition of the ball, said it bore no particular inscription—"just the bruise."

Was this indeed the longest home run ever hit? There is no way of course to be sure, but there was only one accurately measured homer that might have traveled farther. During the Yankees' spring training in 1919, Babe Ruth rifled a shot which writer Tom Meany reports cleared a race track that circled the playing fields of the old Tampa fairgrounds. The distance was measured by some of the sportswriters. They figured it went between 500 and 587 feet, depending on whose memory you use.

In that tape measure game at Washington, Mickey bunted a ball so hard it almost reached second base on the fly. Yet with his great speed—he had been clocked at 3.1 seconds going down to first left-handed—he beat it out. Some wag commented later, "In one game, Mantle hit the longest home run and the longest bunt in history."

In any case, the era of the tape measure had been heroically introduced. And the results generally worked against Mickey.

Later that season Mickey cracked a 485-foot home run in St. Louis, and a 425-foot job in Chicago. "Watching Mickey every day," said teammate Joe Collins, "I still can't quite bring myself to believe he hits those balls the way he does. You know, he hits them as though they don't count if they're under 400 feet."

Equally unrestrained in enthusiasm about Mantle was the manager. Casey Stengel said, "In my opinion, Mantle is the longest right-handed batter since Jimmy Foxx and the longest left-handed batter since Babe Ruth."

With all this you could hardly blame the fans for expecting Mantle to produce a superhuman wallop almost every time he came to the plate. And when he didn't, the fans were not only disappointed, some of them were enraged.

Said one Yankee Stadium bleacherite in the summer of 1953, "Every time he comes up, the Yankee fans start clapping. When he comes up, they take out the tape measures. What's there, only homers? Don't he ever go for base hits? He can run, but why don't he steal bases. He can bunt, but he don't like to bunt. He's nothing. He's overrated."

Even the sportswriters became crabbed toward Mantle. Once, when Mickey struck out, a writer whispered to Red Patterson, "That ball went 60 feet, six inches."

Yet Mickey, if he heard all the noise about him, seemed to be concentrating only on his play—and he was measuring up. By All-Star time in 1953, Mickey was leading the league in hitting, with a .350 average, he was the All-Star center fielder for the American League (he went 0 for 2 in that game), he was developing into the best fielding center fielder in the league. He was doing everything people had expected of him.

Then on August 8, the season went sour for Mickey. Yankee lefty Bob Kuzava was pitching a no-hitter against the White Sox going into the ninth inning when Bob Boyd lined a ball to right center field. Mickey Mantle raced over, desperately trying to haul down the drive and preserve Kuzava's no-hitter. At the last moment, he lunged for the ball, missed, and wrenched his right knee severely. It was the same knee he had injured in the '51 World Series.

Overnight the leg swelled up nastily and Mickey was hardly able to walk. The Yankees already had broken up the pennant race with an 18-game winning streak, but Mantle asked Casey if he could play. Casey let him, until Mickey's pathetic limp and obvious agony forced Casey to bench him in Boston.

From August 8 to the season's end, Mickey was only half a ballplayer. His batting average diminished rapidly, as did his efficiency. The torn cartilage in his right knee killed him as a left-handed hitter. He couldn't get any support when he put his weight on his leg, and he had to cut down on his swing, sacrificing the power that was his chief value to the Yankees. The weakness of his knee also immobilized him at the plate. He found out that he couldn't move fast enough to hit pitches aimed for the outside corner or thrown tight against his fists.

Batting right-handed was different. Mickey was able to shift his weight to his left foot and take a normal cut. In a way, it was robbing Peter to pay Paul.

Mickey's final 1953 statistics show how great a toll his bad knee took. He got into 127 games, had a .296 batting average, hit 21 homers, 24 doubles, 3 triples and knocked in 92 runs. He struck out 89 times.

The Yankees again met the Dodgers in the World Series. The results were the same for the Yankees—they won another world's championship. In 1952 Mickey had hit .345 against the Dodgers. In 1953, against virtually the same Dodger pitchers, Mickey could muster only five hits in 25 at-bats for a dismal .208 average. Yet two of his hits were game-winners.

In the second game batting right-handed against Preacher Roe, he drove a two-run home run that carried the Yankees to a 4–2 victory. In the fifth game, batting left-handed against Russ Meyer, he triggered another Yankee home run with a grand-slammer.

But these blows seemed to be forgotten by the Yankee brass. What manager Casey Stengel seemed to remember was Mickey Mantle striking out eight times, with Carl Erskine fanning him four times in a row.

And Casey let his displeasure be known. "They had the kid cold," Casey said, "and we knew it and we kept telling him he had to cut down his swing and hit down on the ball like we've been telling him all year. The kid's got power enough to hit into the seats just punching-like for the big one. He can bunt enough with his speed to hit .400, but you try to tell him to stop killing it and he don't do it. The way they were pitching him inside, he couldn't see the ball the way he was swinging, and when they gave it to him low and outside he was chasing it. We got to take him in hand and break him of those bad habits."

Yet there was more to it than that. Behind Casey's blast were a couple of incidents during the season that had rankled the crusty old manager. In July of that year, Mickey had pulled a thigh muscle. But he was well enough that evening to appear with some teammates on a television program—the Arthur Murray House Party in which ballroom dancing is featured. Mickey didn't do any dancing, but he was there, instead of being home resting his leg.

Afterward Casey said, "I advised all the players they either better stick to their own jobs or learn this television racket good enough to make a living in it because maybe they'll need it."

Then in September in a game against the White Sox, Mickey was photographed in the outfield chewing gum and blowing bubbles. The next day the picture of Mickey with a huge bubble obscuring his face ran in hundreds of newspapers all over the country.

The bubble gum incident made Mickey some money—his agent Frank Scott later got him a bubble gum endorsement for $1,500—but it did nothing to help Casey's disposition. He was sore at Mantle. He accused Mickey of acting like a kid. Mickey said he'd never do it again.

As soon as the season was over, Mickey went back home. Then in November he checked into a Kansas City hospital to have a damaged cartilage removed from his knee. The operation was performed by Dr. Dan Yancey. After it was over, Dr. Yancey said, "His knee will be as strong as it was before the operation. There will be no loss of action. He won't have to favor the knee after about three months."

This didn't stop Mickey from pursuing his favorite pastimes, hunting and fishing, and the activity set back his recovery. In February, Dr. Yancey had to surgically remove a fluid-filling cyst from the back of Mickey's right knee. During spring training, Mickey very carefully worked himself into shape. By opening day of 1954, Mickey was ready. He was the starting center fielder for the Yankees.

At first it was rough going. His knee was bothering him and he was having trouble getting around on a pitch. In the first two weeks of the season, his batting average was only .167, and he hadn't had a hit against right-handed pitching. But as his knee grew stronger, so did his batting eye. In time he lifted his batting average over .300, began hitting home runs and driving in runs.

And now he had Stengel on his side. Casey began to see what the boy was doing for the Yankees, a boy with delicate legs, too. Mickey would still react temperamentally when things went wrong—he would throw his helmet into the dugout after a strikeout, or lash out at the water cooler with his legs—but only because he was such a highly charged competitor, because he so much craved to win. "He never stops trying for you," Casey said that summer. "That publicity he gets—it's a big burden to a kid. He don't squawk, he just comes out and plays the game every day."

As for flogging the water cooler to death, Casey would just look at Mantle and say, "Boy, that water cooler ain't striking you out."

But he and Mickey began to enjoy a better relationhsip. Once that summer, after Bill Terry, the old Giants' star, had slammed a home run in an Old Timer's game at the stadium, Casey turned to Mantle and said, "Believe me, you'll be mighty glad to be able to do anything like that when you're fifty-five."

Mickey grinned. "Casey," he said, "I'd be very glad to be able to do that now."

Mickey was doing it, but the Yankees weren't. It was not a good year for the club, not a good year that is, as the Yankees speak of good years. They won only 103 games in 1954, more than any other second-place team in history, but eight less than the league-leading Cleveland Indians. It wasn't altogether Mickey's fault that the Yankees lost the pennant. In fact, it was his best year as a Yankee to date.

He did strike out 107 times, which hurt, and he committed nine errors in the field, second only to Jungle Jim Rivera of the White Sox, but he also led the league in assists with 25. And he finished with an even .300 batting average, 102 runs batted in (the first year he had hit in over 100 runs), 27 home runs (also his season high). He led the league in runs scored with 129. Best of all, he missed only eight games of the season. And after it was all over, Stengel announced, "There are only two players on the Yankees for whom I wouldn't consider deals. They are Yogi Berra and Mickey Mantle."

But the critics never let up on Mickey. The fans continued to boo him, and the sportswriters, the same ones who had predicted greatness for him, also took after him. One New York writer, citing the fact that in the month of September (1954) Mantle had hit only one home run, complained that Mantle's "home run exploits are far too infrequent." Another veteran New York baseball writer was even more blunt.

"The fact remains," wrote the writer, "that he is not the ballplayer he had been expected to be. Nor is it certain that he will ever reach that hoped-for pinnacle."

What bothered many of Mickey's professional critics was that the other two New York center fielders had outshone Mickey in every respect. In 1954 Duke Snider of the Dodgers batted .341 with 40 home runs and 131 runs batted in. Willie Mays of the Giants hit .345 with 41 home runs and 110 runs batted in.

Yet Mickey was not discouraged over his showing. He was still only twenty-three, earning $20,000 a year with the Yankees—and his best years seemed to be ahead of him.

He continued to improve in 1955, and he also continued to hear the taunts from the paying customers.

He changed his batting stance a bit at the start of the 1955 season, hoping to cut down on his strikeouts. He crowded the plate a little more, showed a bit more restraint and didn't go after as many pitches. And it began to pay off. In the first month of the season, Mickey drove in 21 runs and hit ten home runs. On May 13, against the Detroit Tigers, he had his biggest day yet as a major-leaguer.

In the first inning he faced right-hander Steve Gromek. Andy Carey was on first with one out. The count went to two balls and two strikes. Mickey dug in and waited for Gromek's next pitch. It came and he was ready. He sent the ball screaming 400 feet into the right-center field bleachers. This gave the Yankees a 2–0 lead.

In the third inning with Hank Bauer on second base, Mickey lined a run-scoring single into center field.

In the fifth inning, Mickey came up batting left-handed

In spite of painful troubles with his legs, Mantle's speed on the base paths helps keep his batting average consistently high.

against Gromek. With a two-ball, no-strike count, Mickey connected and sent the ball into the right-center field bleachers, a 430-foot tape measure job.

In the eighth inning Mickey came to bat right-handed against Bob Miller. On Miller's first pitch, Mickey hit one into the right-center field bleachers, his third home run of the day. The Yankees won the game, 5–2, all five runs driven in by Mickey. More important, it was the first time in American League history that the same player had struck home runs in a game batting right-handed and left-handed.

Later in the season Mickey did it again. Against Baltimore, he hit a home run right-handed off Art Schallock, left-handed off Ray Moore. The homer off Schallock was tinged with irony because Schallock was recalled to the Yankees in 1951 and Mickey was sent to the minors to make room for the pitcher.

In the 1955 All-Star game, Mickey smashed a three-run home run but the National League won, 6–5, in 12 innings.

He finished the season in pain. In a September game against the Red Sox he pulled a thigh muscle. But he still had had quite a season. In 147 games, one more than the previous year, Mickey batted .306, tied for triples with 11, won the home run title with 37 and drove in 99 runs. He made only two errors in the outfield and struck out only 81 times. Another interesting aspect of that year is that Mickey batted .371 right-handed and .279 left-handed.

Because of the thigh injury, the 1955 World Series against the Dodgers was largely a loss for Mantle. The Yankees won the first two games with Mantle out of the lineup. In the third game, Mickey was put back into center.

In the first inning, Mickey went for a fly ball hit by Junior Gilliam. He made a desperate one-handed catch of a ball he could easily have had if his leg had been sound. In the second inning, Stengel shifted Mickey to right field. Batting that inning, Mickey hit a home run. But the Dodgers won the game.

Mickey played in the fourth game, too, and he got a hit, but he was otherwise useless. He stayed out of the last three games except for an unsuccessful pinch-hitting role against Johnny Podres in the seventh game, the game the Dodgers won to become world champions.

It had been another "good" year for Mickey Mantle, but still not the year the experts had envisioned for the man who would be the new Joe DiMaggio. Would he ever? The experts wondered. Everyone wondered. The next year, 1956, Mickey Mantle had the answer for them all.

CHAPTER TEN

GREAT, NOT GOOD

One spring in Florida, there was a discussion of baseball rookies and Fresco Thompson, vice-president of the Brooklyn Dodgers, had this to say.

"You can scout a boy's power and his arm and his speed," Thompson said, "but you can't scout his heart. What's in it you'll never know until the boy is with you and the chips are put on the table."

In a 1953 *Saturday Evening Post* article, the same question was posed about Mickey Mantle. In the story, called "The Yankees' Troubled Ace," the writer, Joe Trimble, tried to explain why Mickey could gain greatness and then again why he could miss it.

"Mickey could blow it himself," the article went on. "He has the physical equipment to become a super star, but he may not have the intangibles that this also takes. This is the big unanswered question about Mantle. So far, he has not demonstrated a willingness to work everlastingly hard to make himself the best. He seems to lack the inner spark of a DiMaggio—that burning desire to excel."

Mickey Mantle was fully aware of these criticisms. A sensitive young man, he knew what most everybody in baseball had predicted for him. And he felt, perhaps unjustly, that he had let people down. He was good, but not great, and he wanted desperately to be great, to excel.

But he also felt deep inside that greatness could be achieved. All he needed was some technical adjustments in his play, some breaks on the field, plus certain intangibles such as poise and confidence, that are part of the growing-up process.

In 1956, the twenty-four-year-old Mantle gained those intangibles. It was the year he came of age.

It was time, certainly. He was going into his sixth season as a major-leaguer. He was a kid no more. He was a family man, with two sons (David had come along to join Mickey, Jr.). In January he signed a contract for about $30,000. At that session he held a conversation with Bill DeWitt, then the Yankees' assistant general manager.

"I was glad to see Yogi get the Most Valuable Player award," Mickey said. "There's no better guy in the world than Yogi. But I'm just wondering. What's a guy have to do to be considered most valuable?"

It was a legitimate question because in 1955 Mickey had outhit Yogi by 34 points, blasted ten more home runs, and driven in only nine less than Yogi.

DeWitt was candid with Mickey. "Maybe," he said, "when the baseball writers are deciding who's been most valuable, they take other things into account. Maybe a ballplayer has to do more than have a good season on the field. Maybe he has to win a little personal popularity. Maybe he has to put out a little effort. Maybe he can't brush off every newspaperman who approaches him or just clam up on him. Maybe he must make a real effort to be more cooperative."

Mantle listened keenly, and he absorbed DeWitt's advice.

Starting in St. Petersburg in spring training, the writers could sense a change in Mickey. For one, he appeared more gracious to them, answering their questions courteously. One reporter came up to Mickey behind the batting cage at St. Petersburg and Mickey volunteered, "We've got some likely looking kids on this squad." The reporter observed, "Mantle for the first time has ceased to regard himself as a kid and was taking on the status of an old hand, and liking it."

Shirley Povich of the Washington *Post* wrote, "It was the new Mickey Mantle, flexing not only in muscles . . . but testing out his new importance as a six-year veteran of the majors."

Mickey also took time to explain to reporters why he felt he must remain as a switch-hitter, despite the clamor in some quarters that he go all the way righty. Remember, Mickey batted 92 points right-handed in 1955 (.371 to .279), and there was a widespread feeling that he might be better swinging righty all the time.

Mickey disagreed. "I've been a switch-hitter all my life," he said. "My father taught me how to hit left-handed so

I'd have an advantage when I batted against all kinds of pitching. Besides, I hit differently right-handed from left. I get a better cut left-handed, but it's a swing that comes up and so I strike out more that way.

"When I hit right-handed," Mickey went on, "my swing is more level. I get more power, and the ball goes farther, even though it looks as though it won't. Those left-handed shots that look as though they're going to go for a mile and drop all of a sudden do that because of the spin the ball gets when I swing upward."

Mickey did look different at bat in the spring of '56. For one thing he worked purposefully at cutting down his strikeouts. In the whole of spring training, he struck out only once, that on a called third strike. He also adjusted his stance to make him less vulnerable to the tight pitch across the letters. "They've thrown me plenty of balls from the belt up inside with plenty of stuff on them and I couldn't do much with this," Mickey explained. "I'm not plumb out of it yet, but I'm hitting that pitch a little better."

He seemed to be hitting *all* pitches better. Mickey had a brilliant exhibition season. In one March game against the Cardinals, he lined a ball towards right-center field. Stan Musial, playing right field, turned and watched the ball sail high over the fence. Afterward Stan said, "No home run ever cleared my head by so much before. The kid looks different this year. He always struck out a lot, but now he's letting bad pitches go. If he hits sixty homers and bats .400, I can't say I'll be surprised."

The feeling began to grow that 1956 would be the year of the tiger for Mickey Mantle. One baseball writer, Joe Reichler of the Associated Press, actually had the nerve to suggest that Mickey might capture the sacred Triple Crown—the batting, home run and runs-batted-in title—*plus* the league's Most Valuable Player award.

Ten days before the start of the season, Mickey bruised his right leg sliding into base and suddenly all the extraordinary predictions about Mantle began to be toned down by the writers. But Mickey was in the opening day lineup for the Yankees at Griffith Stadium, against the Washington Senators. And he indicated right off what kind of a year it would be for Mickey Mantle.

In the first inning, batting left-handed against Camilo Pascual, Mickey celebrated the new season by walloping a 450-foot home run over the center-field wall.

In the sixth inning, with two men on base, Pascual still the pitcher, Mickey came up again, and again he hit a long home run over the center-field wall. President Dwight D. Eisenhower was one of those who rose and cheered as Mickey rounded the bases.

Later, Jerry Coleman, Mickey's teammate on the Yankees, suggested that that opening day explosion might have marked a turning point for Mantle. "It was boom-boom," Jerry said, "and he had two tremendous homers without even trying. It gave him confidence. I've noticed since that he's going with the pitches. If they pitch him inside, he'll pull the ball. But if they pitch him outside, he'll slice to the opposite field. Last year he'd have tried to overpower them by pulling the ball anyway."

Three games later, the Yankees opened at home against the Red Sox. Ike Delock was the pitcher and Mickey crashed another three-run homer. A day later he hit another home run against the Red Sox. Ted Williams, the great Red Sox hitter, was impressed. Ted said, "I see no

Courtesy, *Sport* Magazine

Mickey Mantle is one of those batting stars who always draws other ballplayers as an audience when he takes batting practice.

reason why Mickey can't be a .340 hitter this year and hit forty home runs."

The barrage continued. Mickey hit 16 homers in the month of May, giving him 20 for the Yankees' first 41 games. On May 5 he hit two against Kansas City. On May 18 he hit two against Chicago, one right-handed, one left-handed, sparking the Yankees to an 8–7 victory. On May 30, Memorial Day, he turned in a rare feat.

It was the bottom of the fifth inning at Yankee Stadium, two men were on base, and Mickey came up left-handed against the Washington Senators' Pedro Ramos.

Ramos held the runners, then came in with his pitch. Mickey watching the flight of the ball as it screamed in toward him, bent his knees, dropped his right shoulder slowly toward the ball, clenched his bat, raised it and swung with all the power he could muster—power generated by his legs, back, shoulders, neck and arms. And the ball was propelled high and far toward the right-field roof. For one breath it looked as though it might clear the majestic heights of the gray-green facade, high above the three tiers of grandstand seats. And no one, not even Babe Ruth, had been able to hit one out of Yankee Stadium.

The ball finally struck high on the facade, two feet below the edge of the roof. It was one of the most immense drives ever hit at Yankee Stadium.

Afterward, there was head-shaking from veterans and rookies alike, from non-baseball men and from battle-hardened old pros. Yankee coach Bill Dickey, himself a member of the Hall of Fame and one-time teammate of Babe Ruth, was simply awed by that hit. "I've seen a lot of power hitters come and go," Dickey said, "but Mantle has more power than any man I've ever seen step up to the plate."

"Does that include Babe Ruth?" a reporter asked Dickey.

"I've got to say yes," said the Yankee coach.

Mel Ott, the old Giant star and also a Hall of Famer, was equally impressed with Mickey. "I think Mantle is the most amazing kid in the game. I never have seen so many good qualities. He has strength, speed and good coordination. He's a much improved player over last year, too. You can't fool him very often and, even when he's partly fooled, he's so powerful he's likely to get a hit anyhow."

Where did that power come from? Certainly, there isn't anything extraordinary about a ballplayer who is five foot 11 and a half inches tall, and who weighs 192 pounds. That's average size for a major-leaguer. But don't be fooled by such figures. "Mickey is," said one writer, "built like a blacksmith."

The twenty-four-year-old had a slim waist, but muscular arms and shoulders, an impressive 46-inch torso topped by a pro football lineman's 17-inch neck, and an enormous back. There is an old saying, "If you want to judge a horse or a prize fighter, look at his back." This applies to baseball players, too. One reporter suggested that the more clothes Mantle takes off, the bigger his back seems to get. Yankee players themselves argued over the respective strength of Ted Kluszewski, Gil Hodges or Jackie Jensen, and most of them agreed that Mickey was the strongest man in the big leagues. "Heck," one Yankee player said, "I think he's the strongest man alive."

By early June, Mickey led the league in runs batted in, with 52; in runs scored, with 47; in home runs, with 21; in hits, with 70; in batting average, .407. Rival managers became increasingly perplexed about how to handle Mickey.

One who tried very hard was Lou Boudreau, manager of the Kansas City Athletics. Boudreau, who had devised the famous Ted Williams shift, blocking the right side of the infield, now considered Mantle a more powerful hitter than Ted. So he devised a Mickey Mantle shift.

There is a photograph taken at Yankee Stadium on the night of June 5, the first time the shift was tried on Mantle. The Kansas City shortstop is playing a few steps on the first-base side of second base. The second baseman is playing in short right field. The third baseman is playing center field. The left fielder is playing shortstop. The center fielder is playing in right-center field. The pitcher is Lou Kretlow and Mantle is standing at the plate left-handed. Against Kretlow in the eighth inning of that game, Mickey beat the shift—with a home run into the right-field stands.

On June 18 in Detroit, they rolled out the tape measure again. The score was tied 4–4 in the eighth inning. Gil McDougald opened with a safe bunt. Norm Siebern singled to center. Mickey came up ready to bat left-handed against the Tigers' Paul Foytack.

The count went to two balls and one strike. Then Foytack came in with a fast ball that was well above the letters on Mickey's uniform. If he let it go by, it would have been ball three. Mickey didn't let it go by.

The ball left the park at 360-feet ground distance,

bounding off the roof of the right-field pavilion, which is
110 feet from the field level. Mantle became the second
player in history to hit one out of the Detroit ball park.
Ted Williams was the first one, and the measurers said
that Mickey's drive was hit 20 to 30 feet farther than Ted's.
Incidentally, it won the game for the Yankees.

Finally, it began to dawn on baseball fans that maybe
Mickey Mantle *was* the new Joe DiMaggio. Certainly, the
Yankees had found their drawing card. In the club's second western swing of the season to Cleveland, Detroit,
Chicago and Kansas City, the fans came out in droves. A
night game in Chicago drew 48,345. A Sunday game in
Cleveland drew 41,756. A night game in Detroit drew
47,766. The people were coming out not so much to see
the Yankees, or the home team, but to see Mickey Mantle.

"It's fantastic," commented Casey Stengel. "You know,
when he started turnin' out those homers like he was a
machine, the fans started comin' out to the park early, just
to watch batting practice.

"Used to be I'd sit in the dugout in Kansas City or
Detroit or wherever it might be and all you could see
when he began batting practice was empty stands with
only the ushers watchin' the field. And the only noise
you'd hear would be the players kiddin' and the sound of
the ball meeting the bat. I'd get real lonesome waiting for
the writers to come into the dugout and start me talkin'.

"But now you get to the parks long before the game an'
you have to push through a crowd to get in. By the time
we start hittin' the place is almost filled an' when Mantle
belts one there's as much of a racket an' oohs and aahs as
there is when he hits one during a game.

"He's the first player to bring the fans out early since

Babe Ruth, and you know what? The concession people ought to give him a bonus or help pay his salary or at least keep him in bubble gum because he's the reason they're able to sell so many hot dogs and sody pops an' beer before the game even starts."

In full agreement with the Stengel diagnosis was Will Harridge, president of the American League. "The reaction our office has received to Mantle's homers—distance homers—is positively stunning," Harridge said. "I can't ever recall anything like it. Everywhere I go, in the restaurant, in the elevator and in the barber shop it was Mantle, Mantle, Mantle. They exclaim, 'Mantle's in town,' just like they did for Ruth and Feller. Mind you," Harridge added, "they said Mantle first and the Yankees second."

And this acclaim began to pay off for the country boy from Commerce, Oklahoma. A "Mickey Mantle Enterprises" was organized in Mickey's name for him to make endorsements and advertising testimonials and TV appearances. Mickey endorsed breakfast cereals, hair tonic, cigarettes and a pancake mix called "Batter Up." He joined singer Teresa Brewer in a record called, "I Love Mickey." He appeared on the Perry Como television show and, later in the season, they even made a television show about his life.

What was all this adulation, this sudden burst of fame, doing to Mickey? His friends felt it was maturing him. Said teammate Hank Bauer, "You know, this is quite a strain, everybody nailing him every day and asking him what he thinks about the possibility of breaking Babe's record. I must say he takes it all right. He's not scared any more. He's really grown up all of a sudden."

Said roomie Billy Martin, "Mick is a kid from a small

town who doesn't ever want to become a big city guy. He's most comfortable when he's home with his buddies in Commerce. He feels they understand him better. He's the most modest, unassuming, kindest guy I've ever known."

Mantle himself tried to explain his own feelings. "I'm not much at talking," he said. "I never have a great deal to say. Some people think I'm not friendly because of that. I wish I could be more friendly. I wish I had the disposition of Yogi Berra. But I'm just not built that way."

He continued to do most of his talking with his bat. At the All-Star break, Mickey led the league in batting, with a .371 average; in runs batted in, 71; in runs scored, 70; and in home runs, with 29. He received far more votes than any other player in the voting for the All-Star teams. In the All-Star game at Washington, Mickey hit a home run in a losing cause, the National Leaguers beating the American League, 7–3.

After the All-Star break, Mickey's home run pace slowed a little, but he was still very much in contention for the Triple Crown, which was an achievement he wanted very badly. The Triple Crown had been won only four times in American League history. The last time was 1947 when Ted Williams hit .343, drove in 114 runs and smashed 32 homers. Mickey was well ahead of Williams' pace in all three departments.

On July 30, Mickey hit two home runs against the Cleveland Indians, off Bob Lemon and Bob Feller. On August 4 he hit two more off Detroit's Virgil Trucks. On August 11 he hit his first home run off Baltimore pitching, his 40th homer of the season. The ball was pitched by Hector Skinny Brown. It was a knuckler, al-

most at Mickey's shoe tops, and yet Mickey picked it off
and sent it packing into the upper right-field deck. "Anyone else had hit that," said Baltimore manager Paul
Richards, "it would have been a routine fly. He's a better
player than Babe Ruth." Richards had cause to gush over
Mantle. Mickey had just gone 7 for 12 against Baltimore
pitching. But Richards was sincere.

"Baseball has been looking for a long time for the super
player," Richards said. "Now it can stop looking because
Mantle is that player. He can hit better than anyone else,
he can field better than anyone else, he can throw better
and he can run better. What else is there?"

As the baseball season reached into the heat of summer,
some of that heat, plus the awful pressure on Mantle,
began to touch him. Going to the last day of August,
Mickey had hit 13 home runs in the month. The night of
August 31, the Yankees met the Senators in Washington.
Before the game, Mickey was summoned to the Presidential box. He was introduced to the President of the
United States, Dwight D. Eisenhower. President Eisenhower had decided to come out to the ball park and see
what this Mantle fuss was all about.

"I hope you hit a home run," President Eisenhower
said, "but I hope Washington wins."

Mickey only grinned. In the seventh inning, he hit his
47th home run of the season and President Eisenhower
stood and cheered the most exciting player in the game.
The Yankees disregarded the Presidential order by beating
the Senators, 6–4.

In September, when Mickey needed 14 home runs to
beat Babe Ruth, he slowed down. He hit only five the

entire month. But by this time, he was more concerned about another goal. He wanted very much to be the American League's first Triple Crown winner since 1947.

Mickey confessed, "The last week or so of the season, I was very conscious of it. To tell you the truth, I even dreamed about it at night and thought about it a lot."

For awhile, it looked like he might not win any title, let alone all three. In the first two weeks of September, Mickey had his first real slump of the year. He stopped going for home runs and tried to hit singles. Then he stopped going for singles and tried bunts. And he even had trouble bunting. Manager Stengel and coach Dickey finally convinced Mickey that he was lunging at the ball instead of swinging. When Mickey got back in the groove, he began hitting again.

On September 18, the Yankees played a night game against Chicago at Comiskey Park. A win would clinch the American League pennant. The game went to the top of the 11th inning, the score tied. Mickey Mantle came up right-handed to face Billy Pierce, the White Sox' gutty little left-hander. Mickey drove the ball out of the park, his 50th home run of the season, and his most satisfying. It won the pennant for the Yankees.

On September 28, two days before the end of the season, Mickey led Ted Williams for the batting title, Al Kaline for the runs-batted-in crown and everyone for the homer title. That day, Mickey went 1 for 4; the one hit was his 52nd home run of the season. It gave him a batting average of .353, to Ted Williams' .348. It gave him 128 runs batted in, to 124 for Kaline.

On September 29, Casey rested Mantle. But Mickey got

into the game as a pinch-hitter and he singled in his 129th run.

On September 30, the last day of the season, Mickey grounded out as a pinch-hitter, but drove in his 130th run. He had won the batting title. But Al Kaline had 128 RBI's and the Detroit game was not yet over.

Mickey was too nervous to hang around the stadium for the results. He went to the apartment that he shared with Billy Martin. There, he heard the news that Kaline had been unable to overtake Mickey.

It was official. Mickey was the Triple Crown champion —a .353 batting average, 52 home runs, 130 runs batted in.

That wasn't all. Mickey also led the American League in runs scored, with 132; in base on balls, with 113; in most total bases, 376; in slugging percentage, .705. The only flaw in one of the most remarkable seasons ever enjoyed by a player in the history of baseball was that he had struck out 100 times. And don't think the perfectionist was happy about that.

"I just get anxious so often," Mickey said. "I swing when I shouldn't. The way they pitched me this year, I might have taken 200 walks. But when I get a three ball count and the next one is a strike, I'm ready to swing at the next pitch and I don't care where it is."

Still, it had been a fantastic year and nobody was complaining about Mickey's performance. He had fulfilled every expectation made of him when he first joined the Yankees, a scared kid of nineteen, in that spring of 1951. Now he was great, not good. Now he was Mickey Mantle, king of baseball.

There was, of course, still one unfinished item for

Study in patterns and power: As shadows begin to creep up to the baseline, Mantle breaks for first after connecting with the ball.

Mantle and the Yankees, the World Series. It almost had to be anticlimactic for Mickey. But it wasn't, not really.

It was another down-to-the-wire series for the Yankees against their traditional rivals, the Dodgers from Brooklyn. The Yankees won the Series in seven games. Mickey batted only .250, with six hits in 24 at bats. But three of those hits were home runs as Mickey scored six runs and drove in four. And he had his greatest game on October 3, the day that Don Larsen faced Sal Maglie, the day that Don Larsen made baseball history.

In the fourth inning, the Yankees got their first hit off Maglie. It was hit by Mickey Mantle. It was a home run.

Meanwhile, Don Larsen had been even more stingy. He hadn't allowed a Dodger to reach first base.

The Yankees were leading 1–0 when Gil Hodges came to bat in the top of the fifth. Before Hodges' appearance, the only hard-hit Dodger ball was a liner by Jackie Robinson that caromed off third baseman Andy Carey's glove. But Gil McDougald moved over from shortstop and threw out Robinson. Now Hodges was up, a big, powerful right-handed slugger.

And Gil connected. He hit a low line drive that headed out to deep left-center field, toward the fence. Mickey Mantle raced to his right and back, running diagonally. It seemed to everyone in the stadium that Mantle would never reach the ball—to everyone but Mickey. At the last split second, Mickey reached high, trying to backhand it. The ball caught in his glove and he squeezed it, breaking his stride as he hit the warning track deep in the outfield.

It was the catch that saved Don Larsen's perfect game. The Yankees won, 2–0; Larsen had faced just twenty-seven

Dodgers, and you can't do any better than that. Mickey Mantle had done his part.

A few weeks later, the Mickey Mantle year was confirmed by the experts. By unanimous vote of all 24 selectors, Mickey was named the American League Most Valuable Player for 1956. He became only the second man in history to win the award unanimously. Better still, it established him for what he was—a genuine super star. Now, nobody was selling Mickey short.

CHAPTER ELEVEN

MISERIES, BUT...

It was the busiest winter of his life. It was a winter in which Mickey Mantle saw precious little of his home or his family. It was a winter in which he went all over the country, and beyond, picking up booty.

Athlete of the Year in Dallas, in Tulsa, in Los Angeles; in Rochester, winner of the $10,000 Hickock Belt as the most outstanding professional athlete. Honored speaker at baseball dinners in Chicago, Milwaukee, New York, and all stops, east and west. "About the only thing left for Mantle," commented writer Bill Roeder, "is a trophy for winning the most trophies."

Mickey began to develop poise as a speaker, too. At one gathering in Chicago, Casey Stengel was a spectator and was surprised by the way Mickey handled himself. "He's down in the crowd," Casey said, "and they ask him to come up and speak and he comes to the head table and says, 'This is the first time my manager has heard me speak.' Which is true except that I see him on television and he looks very good. His grammar is very good. He's known all over now. Everywhere he goes they know him and want his autograph. They know him in North and South Dakota."

At another banquet in Milwaukee, Mickey finally got to meet his namesake, Mickey Cochrane. And Cochrane paid Mantle the ultimate tribute.

"This Mickey," said the other Mickey, "will break the Babe Ruth record as sure as I'm standing here."

Mickey spent Christmas in Alaska with Bob Hope entertaining the troops. At one Army base, Mickey came out wearing baby pajamas with a number, .353, written on his back, his 1956 batting average. Bob Hope, who was playing the part of a tough sergeant, pointed to the number and said, "That's your salary up here."

It was 46 degrees below zero outside the air base and Mickey's teeth were chattering, but he grinned.

All in all, Mickey spent over 60 days on the road attending various functions. Not everyone was happy about these activities. The Yankee front office kept a discreet silence, but others spoke out. Frankie Frisch, the old Fordham Flash, said, "Mantle has spent too much time at banquets. A ballplayer should take care of himself during the winter and get plenty of rest."

Mickey's agent, Frank Scott, answered Frisch. "Mickey does rest," Scott said. "He passed up $30,000 to make twenty personal appearances because it was too much."

Still, Mickey had made plenty of money that winter from his various activities—an estimated $59,000, or roughly twice as much as his Yankee salary.

Mickey hoped to right that wrong. He felt he was worth a lot more than the $30,000 the Yankees had given him in 1956. The Yankees felt the same way too, though it took them awhile to come around completely to Mickey's own value of himself.

Originally, the Yankees offered Mickey $42,000, a pretty good raise over '56 but, Mickey felt, not enough. Early in February, he came into New York to attend the annual baseball writers' dinner. Before the dinner, Mickey had a salary meeting with general manager George Weiss and Weiss' assistant Lee MacPhail.

Mickey held out for $65,000.

The Yankees upped their offer to $50,000.

Mickey said no.

The Yankees offered $55,000.

Mickey said no.

Finally, Yankee owner Dan Topping was called in. Topping, it was reported, said to Mantle, "I'm tired of wrangling. Make it sixty and that's final."

Mickey signed his contract happily, thus becoming the highest paid player on the Yankee club and the third highest in Yankee history, behind Joe DiMaggio and Babe Ruth.

Remembering the man who had made it all possible, Mickey spoke wistfully about his dad, Mutt Mantle. "Here I am with a lot of money," Mick said, "the kind of dough Dad never dreamed I would get. I could do a lot of things for Dad, but he isn't around. Think how I feel about that."

Mickey reported to spring training in near perfect shape, though he suffered a bit with shin splints—strains in the muscles of his calf—that he had picked up from playing basketball over the winter. (When he had time for basketball that crowded winter is open to some question.)

His right knee, which had bothered him through the 1956 World Series, seemed to be in good shape. "Mantle's knee is okay," Stengel told reporters at St. Petersburg. "It ain't perfect. I wouldn't kid you about that. But Dr. Gaynor [the Yankee team physician] told me it's stronger."

Watching Mickey hit with his usual vigor in the spring exhibition games, Stengel became enthusiastic. "One of these days," Casey said, "he'll hit a ball so hard it'll burst and all he'll get for his efforts will be a single."

Yet before the Yankees started north, Mickey was out of the lineup. First, he sprained his thumb. Then, while chasing a ball in Miami Stadium, he stepped into a gopher hole and sprained his left foot, just below the ankle.

He limped around the rest of the spring season but by opening day, Mickey was back in the lineup. His hitting was a little different than it had been most of 1956. He either seemed to be forsaking the long ball or unable to blast it out. But he was getting singles and doubles, and he was taking more pitches. He was more selective about the pitches they were giving him. The bases on balls began to add up. So did the hits. By late May, Mickey was batting .368. But he was still having his off days in the field.

On May 22 against the White Sox, Mickey bumped into Elston Howard, who was in left field, causing Howard to drop the ball. In a later inning, Mickey misjudged a fly ball and it fell for a three-base error. Shortly after, he failed to charge a single by Larry Doby of the Indians, permitting Minnie Minoso to score from second base.

When Mantle came into the clubhouse after that game, which the Yankees lost 8–4, he sat at the center table and wept. He wept in frustration over a simple off-day. There had been others in the past, there would be more in the future, but Mickey then, as Mickey now, was unable to reconcile himself to imperfection. It was the one thing he and Mickey's public had in common. Mickey cried at his imperfections; the fans booed at them.

But Mickey was having plenty of good days, too, that season of 1957.

On July 23 the Yankees met the Chicago White Sox. Al Lopez' club was giving the Yankees trouble, running a close second to the Yankees. In the first inning, Mickey doubled. In the third, he singled. In the fifth inning he came up with the bases empty, batting left-handed against right-hander Bob Keegan. Keegan came in with a fast ball and Mickey swung.

The ball started low, but then began to rise—rising, rising, rising, and then smashing high in the right-field bleachers. Many in the crowd of 45,000 thought the ball had gone out of the park. Millions of television watchers felt the same way. The switchboard at Yankee Stadium was clogged for hours as operators explained patiently that the ball had hit two rows from the top. The tape measure was pulled out—465 feet! "One of the hardest hit balls of my career," Mickey admitted.

But that game wasn't over. With a double, single and homer behind him, Mickey had more to do. In the bottom of the seventh the Yankees trailed, 6–4. Elston Howard opened the inning with a triple off of Dixie Howell. He scored on a wild pitch. Jerry Coleman walked. Left-hander Jack Harshman came in to relieve, and he walked Enos Slaughter, Tony Kubek and Gil McDougald in succession, forcing in the tying run. Mickey came to bat with the bases full, score 6–6.

Batting right-handed he smashed a long drive to left. Minnie Minoso ran over, made a leaping stab near the fence. He deflected the ball, preventing a grand-slam homer, but Mickey raced to third with a base-cleaning triple. He had hit for the cycle—single, double, triple, homer—the first time an American Leaguer had hit for the cycle since 1952. And nobody in baseball history had included a 465-foot homer in a cycle performance. Mickey ended the day batting .362, leading the league.

On July 27, Mickey hit his 27th home run of the season against Jim Bunning of the Tigers. It was his 200th major league home run. Babe Ruth had hit his 200th homer when he was twenty-eight. Mickey was still only twenty-five.

By the end of August, Mickey was still very much in contention for the Triple Crown. If he could win the batting, home run and runs-batted-in titles for a second successive year, it would be an unprecedented feat. Mickey hit his 34th home run on August 30. He lagged slightly in runs batted in, but still had a shot at that title, and he was batting in the .350's. The trouble was that he had intense competition from Ted Williams, the thirty-eight-year-old marvel, who was having one of his greatest years.

In an early August three game series in Boston, 101,858 fans turned out to watch the Yankees and Red Sox—or rather to watch Mantle vs. Williams. In the five-week period since the All-Star game, both players had been red hot. Mantle had batted .400 in that period, but Williams had batted .500 and his .387 average was best in the league.

Mickey won the first game. Booed every time he came to the plate by the rabid Red Sox fans, Mickey singled twice and hit a home run. Ted singled once and got two walks.

The next day, Williams evened the battle. He hit a home run with two men on, singled and walked. Mickey had one hit in four tries.

In the third game Ted clinched the duel. He went two for three, a double and a single. Mickey had no hits in two official appearances. When the Series ended, Ted Williams was batting .393, 13 points higher than Mickey Mantle.

The season ended just about that way, too. Williams won the American League batting title with a tremendous .388 batting average. Mickey finished second at .367, the highest average of his career. He had hit 34 home runs, driven in 94 runs and was walked 146 times—high in the American League.

It was not as good a season as 1956, but it was second best in Mickey's major league career. And he accomplished all this despite handicaps that would have put a lesser man in bed.

Early in September, Mickey came down with a case of shin splints. He played off and on, when the Yankees needed him to ward off a late challenge by the White Sox, but he played in pain. "It aches all the time," Mickey said. "It hurts when I run and it hurts between innings."

Those of us who are writers, or lawyers, or accountants, or students, or truck drivers, if we hurt our legs, we go to the doctor, he tells us what to do and we do it. With Mickey Mantle it is not that simple. Often, the only cure for what ails him is rest, total rest, even immobilization of his legs. How do you tell a ballplayer fighting for a pennant that he has to lie down for two weeks?

The pain had actually begun late in August when the Yankees were in the West. In one game against the Senators, Mickey missed a couple of fly balls that he would easily have gotten to if he could run. His 34th home run on August 30 was his last of the year simply because he could not get the proper traction from his weak legs. The pitchers, taking advantage of this, threw at his knees, making him jump back awkwardly, then curved him over the outside corner. Or they'd fire the ball high and tight, where he usually pulled them into the upper deck. Only with a bad leg, he couldn't pull anything except possibly another muscle.

His legs felt so bad, in fact, that one evening Mickey had to be carried out of a car to a restaurant. His legs had tightened up on him.

What are "shin splints"? Medical men are split on the term. One doctor explained it this way: "What is generally referred to as 'shin splints' is nothing more than what I like to call 'wear-and-tear trauma.' Translated, this means that, more and more, Mickey's legs are starting to wear down. There are two factors that contributed to this kind of pain Mickey suffered: arterial spasms in the calves of the legs; and stretching and straining of the attachments connecting muscle and bone. It is hard to distinguish between these two, to find out exactly what the pain is coming from. All we know is that it comes from too much pounding on those legs and that only rest will ease the pain."

Let us assume that Mickey was not bothered with shin splints. His legs would still be suspect. Before every game, Mickey dresses like a mummy. His left ankle, the one with osteomyelitis, is carefully bandaged. On his right leg, below the knee to high on the thigh, he wears a huge swath of tape, to protect the vulnerable knee and weak hamstring muscle.

"Of all the ballplayers I can recall," commented a doctor, "this boy has the absolute worst trouble. Not even Joe DiMaggio had it as bad because with Joe the heel spur came late in his career. Do you realize what a tremendous competitor Mickey must be and what talent he must have to have come so far?"

With this background of injury, with his legs bothering him more than they ever had in his career, Mickey went into the 1957 World Series against the Milwaukee Braves. And almost immediately, he hurt himself again.

In the first inning of the third game, Mickey was on second base, Berra on first. Pitcher Bob Buhl tried to pick Mickey off base. He wheeled and threw the ball into center field. Braves' second baseman Red Schoendienst fell heavily on Mantle's right shoulder trying to make the play.

The shoulder started to pain as Mickey went out on the field. But he played on. He singled in the third inning. In the fourth, with Tony Kubek on base, Mickey came up left-handed and hit a gigantic home run into the right-center field bullpen.

Mickey played the fourth game, but could barely swing

the bat. He sat out the fifth and sixth games. But Casey Stengel, in a move of desperation, inserted Mickey into the deciding seventh game. Mickey managed a single, but it was not enough to prevent the Milwaukee Braves from beating the Yankees and becoming new World Champions.

In 19 official at-bats, Mickey had hit .263. It was far from his best World Series, but all was forgotten several weeks later when announcement was made of the Most Valuable Player in the American League. The winner: Mickey Mantle. For the second consecutive season, Mickey had won the biggest bauble in baseball. Neither Joe DiMaggio, nor Ted Williams, Mickey's closest competitor in 1957, had ever won the award two years in a row. Despite all his miseries, despite his aching shoulder and his sore legs, Mickey felt good all over.

CHAPTER TWELVE

DOWNHILL SLIDE

A winter of hunting and fishing and golf, and more resting than he had done the year before, was a tonic to Mickey. He reported to the Yankees' spring training camp at St. Petersburg in fine shape, only a few pounds overweight. He had received a $10,000 raise from the Yankees and was now making $70,000 a year, better than anyone in the American League except Ted Williams. He had a good spring, too. He batted over .300 and hit eight exhibition game home runs. He seemed to be at peace with himself and at peace with the world.

But not everything was right.

Physically, Mickey had problems. His legs bothered

him, especially his right knee. His right shoulder, injured in that World Series collision with Red Schoendienst, still pained him. He had trouble swinging left-handed because of the soreness. He had also developed an allergy. But he tried to keep these miseries to himself.

"I'm just not hitting," Mickey said. "No reason for me getting out of the lineup. I'm okay."

In the first two months of the season, New York writers and the manager, too, grumbled about Mickey's performance. Mickey hit his fourth home run of the season on May 20. He didn't hit his fifth until June 2. But he hit a sixth the next night with two men on base, and a seventh on June 4, and an eighth, an inside-the-park job, on June 5. Four home runs in four days. That matched his best previous streak, which took place in 1957.

Stengel expressed the wish that Mickey could move with more consistency, but he was also critical of the way pitchers were throwing to Mantle. "I think it's a shame the way they pitch to this kid," Casey said. "I ain't crying, believe me, but it doesn't please me to see the hurlers throw it at his knees, his shins, his ankles. Mantle and my club are lucky that he is so quick on his feet, that he can get away from them nasty throws. I don't believe that any other batter in this league has to contend with that kind of pitching.

"One of these days," Casey said, "a wise-guy pitcher throwing at Mickey's knees and shins will hurt him and then the pitcher will yammer that it was an accident. Accident my foot. Not the way they are working against the kid."

Looking at Mantle's statistics by mid-June of 1958, it was apparent that something was very wrong. In 1957

Mickey had batted .342 left-handed, .414 right-handed, with 26 homers lefty, 8 homers righty, 56 strikeouts left-handed, 19 strikeouts right-handed.

By June 18, 1958, Mickey was batting .228 left-handed, with 8 homers, 15 runs batted in and 44 strikeouts. Right-handed, he was batting .476 with 4 homers, 13 RBI's and five strikeouts. (Note, though, that Mickey appeared 149 times at bat left-handed, only 42 right-handed.)

Finally, Mickey had to admit that his shoulder was bothering him. "I have had a catch in the shoulder," Mickey said. "It doesn't let me take my regular cut at the ball swinging lefty. It feels like a muscle pull, but I really don't know what it is."

In any case, the pain got so bad that Mickey was forced to visit a doctor in Cleveland. He began taking diathermy treatments. And, again, he turned down all suggestions that he bat only right-handed.

"I was brought up to hit both ways," Mickey said. "I don't see how I can learn some other way now."

By the All-Star break, Mickey had struck out a whopping 55 times left-handed. He seemed in danger of breaking all strikeout records. Baseball fans in New York, as well as the other American League cities, had little sympathy for Mickey. They were booing him worse than ever. A feature story in *The New York Times* by Gay Talese tried to come to grips with the question.

"Every time he drives up to Yankee Stadium," wrote Talese, "he is mobbed by a pack of young baseball fanatics. If he does not stop to sign autographs, some teenagers squirt ink into his clothing.

"On Friday, after the doubleheader with Washington, a

girl of thirteen jumped at Mantle as he got out of the cab. She punched him, began to pull his short, blond hair, and slapped him until he swatted her off and bulldozed his way towards the stadium's player entrance.

"In the dressing room before the game, Mantle was smoldering quietly. He said he did not mind all the abuse from hecklers and that 'if they bothered me, I would not be where I am.' Then he turned away.

"At 11:50 A.M., Mantle began batting practice. Out in the bleachers, a stumpy, bald-headed man yelled, 'Look, here comes the All-American out. . . .'

"Then, just before game time, Mantle's name came over the public address system; there was grand applause, and yet easily heard was the undercurrent of booing.

"Why do people boo Mantle at Yankee Stadium?

"Because of a shortage of psychiatrists at the stadium on Friday, some non-professional views were obtained. Casey Stengel does not understand the boos, but believes they come from older fans—not from children. Yet, some teen-agers, just as the thirteen-year-old girl who pulled his hair before the game, claim, 'We don't like Mickey. He's stuck-up.'

"A Yankee press agent pointed out that the modest, somewhat shy Oklahoman is frequently cheered away from the stadium more than he is at the stadium this season. It is also pertinent to note that Yogi Berra, hitting .222—80 points lower than Mantle—never is booed at the stadium. . . .

"A baseball writer, a bit cynical at the moment, said that Mantle is booed because he is the Yankees' 'king.' Sinister anti-Yankee fans thrive on booing the king. Yet the Cardinals' 'king,' Stan Musial, is never booed. Lou Gehrig was hardly ever booed.

"Ruth was booed," the writer went on, "but never maliciously. DiMaggio was not booed much either. They don't boo Berra, because he's a great politician, the greatest baby-kisser in baseball today. Somehow, the name Yogi Berra is warm. He's so ugly you can't help loving him."

There was one other factor that went unmentioned in the column. That is, that Mickey's intense will to win is so obvious, his self-hatred is so obvious when he does things wrong, that fans simply go along with him. When Mickey sulked out loud, the fans sulked out loud right with him. A Ruth, a DiMaggio, a Musial could take their small defeats in stride. Mickey Mantle never could, never will.

In a game at Yankee Stadium in late August, Mickey hit a soaring drive that headed towards the right-field bullpen. But Al Kaline ran back and made a leaping catch, robbing Mickey of a home run. When Mickey returned to the dugout, he went for his favorite target— the water cooler. He whacked it so hard with his left foot that its front panel was knocked off, revealing all the machinery. A reporter in the press box trained his binoculars on the scene.

"That's the first time I ever saw what the inside of a water cooler looked like," he said. "Hey," he said, "there's a sheet that looks like printed instructions inside."

"What does it say?" asked another reporter.

"It says, don't subject this machinery to unnecessary shock."

Despite such self-abuse, Mickey was not really having a bad season. Late in August he lifted his batting average over .300, and his home run output had increased. The Yankees at one time that year held a 17-game lead. But they won only 25 out of their last 44 games. It was enough to win a pennant, but it had the Yankee front office worried.

On the last day of the season, batting under .300, Mickey got three singles in four trips, which made his final average .304. He also led the league in home runs with 42, his second best total as a Yankee. He drove in 97 runs, more than any other Yankee. He had 128 walks, 307 total bases. But he also struck out 123 times, a Yankee record.

In the World Series against the Braves, it wasn't much better. Mickey had one good game, the second in which the Yankees swamped the Braves, 15–5. In his second appearance at the plate, Mantle stepped in against Lew Burdette. The crafty Braves' right-hander hollered, "Watch out, he might try to drag a bunt down the first-base line."

Mickey slammed the ball over the fence.

His next time at bat, Mickey again heard Burdette holler to his Braves teammates. "Look out, he might drag—*again.*"

This time Mickey hit a two-run home run over the right-center field fence, and he laughed all the way around the bases.

Those were the only runs he drove in the whole Series, and his only home runs. Mickey ended with a .250 batting average, 6 for 24. But the Yankees, after being down three games to one, regained their championship miraculously, winning the last three from the Braves. And Mickey Mantle was a happy man.

"It was the biggest thrill I ever had in baseball," he said. "When you're down three games to one, it's hard to make yourself think you'll win. But we did."

That winter, an old rival, Jackie Jensen, now with the Red Sox, was named Most Valuable Player in the American League.

That winter, too, Mickey did some rearranging of his personal life.

He bought a luxurious ranch home in a suburb of Dallas, Texas, and moved his whole family. One of the reasons Mickey moved to Dallas was to be near his new 32-lane, $650,000 bowling alley. But he joked that he had left Oklahoma for other reasons.

At a press conference in Dallas, Mickey told reporters, "Texas has some good football teams now, so I thought I'd move down here where I could root for Southern Methodist."

Mickey was loose and easy at that press conference but that winter, as it turned out, was one of the most uncomfortable of his life.

It started, in a minor way, by a remark of Casey Stengel's to sportswriters. Asked to name the greatest players he had ever handled, Stengel listed them this way:

"DiMaggio first, then Berra, then Hank Bauer." Mickey Mantle's name was nowhere on Casey's list.

As if that weren't bad enough—and Mickey had to feel hurt by Stengel's obvious snub—a Yankee teammate got into the act. In mid-January, outfielder Hank Bauer addressed a dinner in St. Paul, Minnesota. Here is what he supposedly said:

"Mantle is inclined to sulk when he's not whole hog. And, when he's in a slump, he tends to let down on himself and the club.

"If you had 25 Mantles on the team, you wouldn't be sure to win the pennant. I found that the only way to win is for everybody to give 100 percent for the team."

Later, Hank Bauer denied that he had made such remarks. But they stood. Back in Dallas, Mickey tried to laugh them off. "He may not be too far wrong," Mickey said. "I'm not exactly the best fielder in the world. But I'm not alarmed. Bauer is one of my best friends on the club. If he said it, I don't think he meant it that way."

Yet Mantle was deeply hurt by the remarks. A couple of weeks later the boom was lowered on him by the Yankee front office.

Mickey received his contract. It called for him to take a $10,000 *cut*. He had hoped to be raised a few thousand, and he had said he wanted $15,000 more. But a *cut*. It was unthinkable.

Yet it was true. The Yankee management, dissatisfied with the performances of a number of Yankee players, had asked Mantle, Gil McDougald, Moose Skowron and Yogi Berra, all to take cuts. General manager George Weiss explained, "At current salary rates, players who had poor seasons must be reduced to keep pay at a sensible level."

Was 1958 a poor season for Mickey Mantle? Well, his batting average was lower than 1957, but he still hit over .300. And he did lead the league in homers with 42, eight more than he had hit in 1957, and he drove in three more runs than he had in '57. And he played when a lesser man would have begged off.

Furious, Mickey made some bitter statements. "I don't report until I get exactly what I want," he spouted. And he sat back stubbornly and waited. He was bitter not simply because of the cut itself, but because of the blow to his enormous pride.

He wasn't the only bitter one about a pay cut. Whitey Ford, Mickey's friend, said, "If they're trying to cut him so bad and it looks like maybe he won't play, you can bet me there are guys on this club willing to chip in and make up the difference. We need him."

The war of nerves ended on February 28, the day before spring training. Mickey Mantle was not cut in salary. He did in fact receive a $2,000 raise. He showed up at the press conference announcing the signing in a beaming mood. He wore a navy blue silk suit with narrow lapels, a white shirt and light striped tie. He joked with writers.

"You wrote a bad story about me this winter," he said to one reporter.

"What was bad about it?" the sportswriter asked.

"You had me using all those double negatives," Mantle said.

"Don't you use double negatives?"

"Sure I use 'em," Mickey said. "But you don't have to print 'em."

He joked, but the bad taste was still in his mouth. And it would be reflected in the year of 1959, which was the most frustrating of Mickey's baseball life.

It started on April 12, just before the opening of the season. He hurt his right shoulder making a throw from center field to first base. The shoulder ached on and off until late July when the summer sun finally baked it out. He chipped a bone in his right forefinger in May. He sprained an ankle in June. And, of course, there were the legs. Otherwise, he was fine.

Mickey was determined to improve on his '58 showing. Just before opening day he told his plans for the season.

"I'm going to steal more," Mickey said. "They walk me too much. A walk and a steal is like a double. Maybe I'll get more good balls to hit if they know I'm going to steal."

But with the bad shoulder, Mickey got off to a slow start. And the Yankees did, too. On May 20, the team fell into last place. Nothing like that had ever happened to a Casey Stengel Yankee team before. Mickey's batting average was .275.

Al Lopez, whose Chicago White Sox were putting on the steam in the American League, laid the blame for the Yankee collapse on Mantle. "Mickey is the most talented, natural ballplayer I've ever seen," Lopez said. "But he hasn't capitalized fully on his gifts. Now he's getting heavy and he's lost some of his speed. In 1956 and 1957, his two best years, he was in there swinging. Last year he took too many pitches and his hitting suffered.

"I don't like to say this about any ballplayer, especially a great one like Mickey," said Lopez, "but I don't think he'll last very long as a top-notch star."

Shortly after these remarks, Mickey had the pleasure of hitting a tape measure home run against Mr. Lopez' White Sox. The ball landed ten-rows deep into the upper deck of the Yankee Stadium 450 feet away. "Best one I've hit in two years," Mickey said, smacking his lips. "I knew it when it left the bat."

Early in June, after striking out three times in a row against Baltimore, Mickey got hot. In the next seven games he batted .522. One day Mickey drove in six runs. Another day, he made five consecutive hits, one of them a home run. He stole nine bases in ten tries. He was fielding as well as he had ever fielded in his career.

Between May 25 and June 29, Mickey batted .326 with 14 home runs and 36 runs batted in.

On a Sunday doubleheader in July when the Yankees twice beat the White Sox—Al Lopez again—Mickey went two for four in both games. In the first game, he doubled in the fifth inning, stole third and scored on a sacrifice fly. In the second game his double in the third and his home run off relief ace Turk Lown in the fifth drove in three runs.

Was it Mantle's fault that the Yankees could not seem to rise from fifth place? It was not. Before spraining his ankle and reinjuring his shoulder, on June 16, Mickey was blasting away at a 40-home run, 100 runs batted in pace. Yet the Yankees were in fifth place. It wasn't Mickey who was having the poor year, it was the Yankees.

Yet the pressure grew on him. It was a combination of his own physical injuries, plus bad seasons certain of his teammates were having, that broke Mickey. The pressure grew on him all season long, piling up with every game played, and every game lost, and the distance between first place and the Yankees growing steadily. The job was impossible. He couldn't carry a 25-man club alone. He had to go for the long ball every time.

And so the bat's whiplash became more fierce, more desperate. Mantle kept pressing, just as the pressure kept pressing, and the whiplash met nothing but futility, mounting futility as the dismal season progressed. And when the Yankees' position became helpless, Mickey would not have been human had he not let himself finally drift into a tailspin.

He was striking out a lot. In three awful July weeks, Mickey batted only .238 with no home runs. He had a little better August. In one doubleheader he powered his 23rd home run in the first game, his 24th in the second, plus a double that streaked on a line 461 feet before it struck the center-field fence.

But it was no go for the Yankees. They finished in third place in the American League, winning only 79 games, and Mickey Mantle was booed more than he had ever been in his life.

At Yankee Stadium, he was jeered when he struck out, and the fans made jokes. "It's hot," one of them shouted down to Mantle a day in August. "Send us a little breeze, Mick." And when the big yellow bat whiplashed and hit only air, the fans rocked with high-cackled laughter and a chorus of boos heaped down on Mickey as he trotted out to his position.

Even when he got a hit, even when that hit was a thin streak of white flying on an unbending line deep into the black mass of fans in the upper tier of right field or into the bullpen in left center, they got on him. "Oh, you lucky bum, you! What'd they throw you, a fish?"

But take a closer look at Mickey's 1959 record. On the negative side, he did strike out 121 times, more than anyone in the modern history of baseball except for Steve Bilko, who once had 125, and Vince DiMaggio who holds the record with 126. One disgruntled cynic mumbled, "If

Mantle's legs hold up, he'll set all kinds of records—strike-out records, I mean."

The Mantle haters also pointed to his batting average, .285, a new low for Mickey, not befitting his $72,000 salary. Sure, if Mickey had turned just eleven of those at-bats into hits, he would have finished at .304—his 1958 average—and the Yankees still wouldn't have won the pennant. As it was, his .285 mark was tenth highest in the league. His 31 home runs represented his major league average and no other American Leaguer who had 30 or more home runs had a higher batting average than Mickey.

Mickey's slugging percentage was third highest in the league, his total bases third highest. He drove in 75 runs.

He also had 21 stolen bases, second high in the league. He also led all outfielders in defensive play with a .995 figure, just two errors. And only Jim Landis and Al Kaline made more put-outs.

Yet he was Mickey Mantle and so he should have done better.

That's what they all said, the amateurs and professionals. One baseball writer allowed that Mickey was the most disappointing hitter in the American League. Why? Because he suffered "no important injuries." That's what the man said. Another writer suggested that because Mantle had incorporated himself, he was paying too much attention to his business, not enough to his baseball. Perhaps if Mickey had made his business more of a diversion from baseball, he might have given a fresher effort to the game.

The truth was simple. Mickey Mantle had had an off-year. Every ballplayer since creation had had bad years in his career. Babe Ruth had bad years. Lou Gehrig had bad years. Joe DiMaggio had bad years. Stan Musial had bad years. Ted Williams had bad years. Mickey Mantle had his bad year in 1959. The reason it seemed *so* bad was that the Yankees lost a rare pennant. It was *so* bad for Mickey because, as Casey Stengel always said, "Mickey could lead in everything—anything they put in the books. Not just one year. Every year."

The trouble with a downhill slide is to try and break it. That's the toughest thing in the world. Mickey's downhill slide began in 1958, after midseason, and it almost exactly paralleled the downhill slide of the Yankees as a team. Between August of 1958 and June of 1960, the Yankees lost 120 of 239 games. Then they put on the brakes.

And so did Mickey Mantle.

CHAPTER THIRTEEN

NEW DAY COMING

Again for Mickey Mantle, the winter was not a happy period, that winter of 1959–60.

When he received his first contract, Mickey was asked to take a cut of $17,000. That would put him back to $55,000. Mickey thought he had read it wrong and he sent it back. The Yankees said it was no mistake. "That's what you're worth," they said.

It was like a slap in the face. Mickey became a serious, determined holdout. When spring training officially opened in St. Petersburg on March 1, Mickey was absent. Neither he nor general manager George Weiss would budge from their positions.

But on March 10, nine days after the official start of practice, Mickey flew into St. Petersburg. He found it unbearable being away from baseball. He and George Weiss immediately went into a conference. When it was over, Mickey came out with a $65,000 contract, a $7,000 reduction. He was grim-faced. "They gave me a pretty stiff cut," Mickey said as he donned his old No. 7 uniform. "I'm surprised the number wasn't trimmed to 6¾."

Mickey promised he would be out to do his best. "What I'm interested in now," he said, "is getting in shape and having a good season after the lousy one I had last year. I began to press, got mad at myself and then everything went wrong. I honestly believe I'm going to have a good year. Physically, I feel better than I have in years."

But it didn't show at first. Mickey rounded into shape slowly, two slowly for the Yankees. In the first two months of the 1960 season, while the club was losing 20 of its first 41 games, Mickey was locked in the worst slump of his career. And it was hurting.

The mob was on him worse than ever. One day, after catching the final out in a game against Washington, Mickey came directly to grips with his tormentors.

He was trotting toward the dugout when 100 or more fans leaped out of the stands and started towards Mantle. Mickey swung his arms and shoulders, trying to fight off the crowd. They were after his glove, his cap, his shirt. Suddenly, someone threw a punch. It landed near Mickey's jaw. Fortunately, he kept on his feet and pushed to the safety of the clubhouse. X-rays showed no break, but Mickey was on a soft diet for four days.

So the Yankees stumbled as they waited for Mickey to deliver them out of the wilderness. "When he hits, we

Courtesy, *Sport* Magazine

The famous "M and M" hitters of 1961, Roger Maris and Mickey Mantle, flank business agent Frank Scott. Early in the season it appeared as though both or either would break Babe Ruth's 60 home run record. Mantle fell short, but Maris hit 61 for a new (but longer season) record.

move," said pitcher Art Ditmar. Suddenly, in early June, Mickey began to move.

His batting average was .225 at the time, the Yankees were in fourth place. But Mickey got hot. In 17 games he hit .422. In one 11-game stretch, he hit eight home runs. Behind Mickey's rampage, the Yankees charged into first place, winning 14 of 17 games.

One Mantle home run will demonstrate the lift he gave the club. In a game against the Indians, the Yankees fell behind 3–1. But they tied it up going into the last of the eighth. Mickey led off that inning batting right-handed against Dick Stigman. He took a strike. Then he swung and missed a pitch by two feet. With a two-strike count, Mickey hitched up his trousers, bent in and connected on a Stigman fast ball. He lined it into the left-field seats to give the Yankees a 4–3 victory.

One thing that seemed to be helping Mickey now was the presence of a new No. 4 batter in the Yankee lineup. Roger Maris. Maris was acquired in trade from Kansas City over the winter and he was helping to take some of the pressure off Mickey. But Maris was having his own troubles with Mickey batting ahead of him.

In one Detroit game, Mickey hit a home run off Frank Lary. When Maris got up, he was brushed back by Lary. A few innings later, Mickey hit another home run off Lary. The first pitch to Maris following Mantle's blast went over the top of Roger's head.

The day after he hit those two home runs off of Frank Lary, Mickey was complaining about his right knee. "It hurts worse now than it has all year," he said. "It's loose. All the ligaments are torn loose."

During the summer, Mickey was still batting under .300 and he was still making simple mistakes. Once he struck out and stomped back to the dugout, not realizing that the catcher had let the ball go behind him. Another time he ran on a fly ball, mistakenly thinking that there were two out. He was doubled off first base.

But the most damaging moment, the one that possibly changed his whole career, came on August 13 against Washington when, with Roger Maris on first base and only one out, Mickey hit a ground ball to third and failed to run the ball out. He thought there were two outs, the Senators made the double play and the Yankees lost a ball game. And then Casey Stengel, in a rage, pulled Mickey out of the lineup.

It was a moment of deep humiliation for Mickey as we have tried to indicate in the first chapter of this book. It also changed his outlook. He was determined to atone for this lapse. And he did. He began hitting home runs and driving in runs and he sparked the Yankees to 15 consecutive victories.

The Yankees were pennant winners again and—miracle of miracles—the fans had stopped booing Mantle. Whether it was the presence of a young and able rival, Roger Maris, in the lineup, whether it was Mickey's clutch hitting down the stretch, whether it was the public dressing down leveled at him by manager Stengel, the fans were now *with* Mickey.

He ended up leading the league in home runs with 40, one more than teammate Maris. Twenty of Mickey's homers had either won games or set up wins. Mickey led the league in runs scored with 119. He drove in 94 runs.

He fielded superbly, making only three errors despite an aching shoulder and a bad leg. And now, a happy Casey Stengel let himself go in evaluating Mantle.

"It's amazin' what he has done," Casey said, "and him a cripple playing on one leg. He's twice as good a fielder this year as he ever was before. The wind or anything else don't bother him, and he chases the ball and he's sure on a catch. And he has hit the home run in the late innings of second games of doubleheaders and it's a good thing I didn't take him out for a rest in second games or I'd have been trimmed.

"He is exceptional going home from first on a double, crippled and all. He can steal a base whenever I ask him to. He has had to overcome being a strikeout king and to do that he's been taking maybe too many pitches, and when you're like that you strike out on one pitch anyhow and those pitchers have all been very careful pitching to him. But you notice, he's got over 100 walks, too."

Then Stengel compared Mantle and Maris. "At the halfway mark," he said, "my most valuable player was Roger Maris. He still is one of my top producers. Hitting or slumping, he never has given me a bad performance in right field. But Mantle has worked hard and hustled hard and now I've got to say he's my most valuable player."

Now, for the first time since 1956, Mickey was going into a World Series in sound shape. And a lot of experts looked for Mickey to set the way in the World Series. Mike Higgins, manager of the Red Sox, said, "He seems to be set to do big things." And veteran baseball writer Dan Daniel predicted, "There is a strong feeling around the American League and doubtless in Pittsburgh, too, that Mickey Mantle will break out in the World Series."

And so it was.

It didn't start out that way, though. The Pirates won the first game of the 1960 World Series, 6–4, and Mickey was without a hit. He went 0 for 3. In the second game Mickey came up in the first inning and struck out, his third successive strikeout. Then he walked before stepping in against left-hander Fred Green in the fifth inning. Roger Maris was on first base.

Batting right-handed against Green, Mickey smashed a rising liner that soared into the right center-field seats over the 375-foot mark. Later he said, "When I struck out that first time, I figured here comes another one of those games —four strikeouts. I'm the guy who can do it—you know that."

In the sixth, Mickey struck out again. But in the seventh he faced Joe Gibbons, one of the fastest pitchers in the National League. Mickey timed a fast ball perfectly. It headed toward the center-field fence. Bill Virdon, the Pirate center fielder, bolted for the fence.

"I knew I'd never catch it," Virdon said later. "The ball got out there faster than any ball I've ever seen."

Majestically, Mickey's wallop cleared the ivy-cluttered wall at the 435-foot sign. He became the first right-handed batter ever to hit one out of that area at Forbes Field.

The Yankees slaughtered the Pirates in that game, 16–3. Mickey had two walks, two home runs, three runs scored and five runs batted in.

He continued his hitting in the third game, won by the Yankees 10–0. He singled in the first inning, later scoring. He singled in the second inning. In the fourth inning, with Whitey Ford on base, Mickey came up against Fred Green again. This time he drove a 430-foot homer into the left-field bullpen. In the fifth inning, Mickey doubled into the stands along the right-field line. They finally got Mickey in the seventh on a strikeout. But it was a four for five day—home run, double and two singles.

Mickey went hitless in the fourth game, won by the Pirates 3–2. He went hitless in game No. 5, too, though he walked three times. And the Pirates won another, 5–2. In the sixth game, which the Yankees won 12–0, Mickey drove in two runs with a single. He had strained his groin in the fifth game, but he played on.

So it came down to game No. 7, one of the weirdest and wildest World Series games ever played. It was a magnificent game for Mickey Mantle.

The Pirates jumped to a 4–0 lead in the early innings. Vern Law seemed unbeatable. Mickey flied out and singled in his first two appearances. It was 4–1, Pirates going to the top of the sixth and it looked like a World Championship for Pittsburgh. But the Yankees weren't through.

Bobby Richardson singled. Tony Kubek walked. Then relief ace Elroy Face came in for Law. Roger Maris fouled out to Don Hoak, but Mickey came up and drilled a single through the box and into center field, scoring Richardson. Then Yogi Berra came up and hit a three-run home run, and the Yankees had the Pirates 5–4.

In the top of the seventh, the Yankees scored two more, making it 7–4. But then the Pirates rallied courageously in the bottom of the eighth.

Gino Cimoli batted for Face and singled. Bill Virdon came up. He hit a ground ball towards Tony Kubek. It looked like a double play. But the ball hit a pebble, bounced up and struck Kubek in the throat, knocking him down. That put men on first and second. Groat singled in Cimoli. Bob Skinner sacrificed. Rocky Nelson flied out. **Roberto Clemente beat** out an infield chopper, scoring Virdon. And catcher Hal Smith hit a home run over the left-field wall. It was 9–7, Pirates.

Desperation. Top of the ninth inning, two runs behind, a world championship at stake. But the Yankees do not quit. Bobby Richardson led off with a single against Bob Friend, the new Pirates' pitcher. Dale Long pinch-hit a single. Left-hander Harvey Haddix was called in. He got Maris to foul to catcher Smith. Then Mickey came up.

He promptly lined a single to right-center scoring Richardson and sending Long to third. That set up a play that would long be remembered.

One man out, McDougald on third, Mantle on first, Yogi Berra up. Berra sent a one-hop screamer just inside the first-base line. First baseman Nelson had come off the bag with Mantle, but with a fine lunge he managed to backhand the drive and step on first to retire Berra.

Now Nelson wheeled to tag Mantle, who stood frozen some ten feet from first—a dead duck. But before Nelson could make a move, Mickey had recovered, reacting instantaneously. He scrambled under Nelson's glove with a fall-away slide and made it back to first as McDougald raced home with the tying run.

"It was a good play on Mantle's part," said Casey Stengel. "He thought quick."

Casey was speaking those words in sorrowful tones in the Yankee clubhouse after that game, after Bill Mazeroski had hit the home run in the bottom of the ninth that had sent the Yankees crashing to a stunning loss of their world championship. Casey sat there and lauded Mickey Mantle.

Where was Mickey? He was hunched down in front of

his locker, head down, tears streaming down his checks.

"I was so moved looking at Mickey," said Yankee publicity director Bob Fishel, "that I felt like crying, too."

Mickey was crushed. "This is the first time we lost a Series when we should have won," he muttered.

But it hadn't been Mickey's fault. He had had his best World Series ever. He batted .400, 10 for 25. He scored 8 runs, drove in 11, walked eight times and hit three of the longest home runs in Series history.

A couple of weeks later the Most Valuable Player was announced for the American League. Roger Maris won it, beating out Mickey by three votes.

But there was a new day coming.

CHAPTER FOURTEEN

THE LEADER

An event of extreme importance to Mickey Mantle took place in New York City on October 20, 1961. The Yankees had called a press conference in the Savoy Hilton Hotel. Casey Stengel had been fired, as Casey himself had abundantly made clear. The new Yankee manager was to be introduced to the press.

Ralph Houk came striding into the room, all six foot, one inch, 200 pounds of him, his dark hair glistening, his round face set off by the perpetual cigar in his mouth. And for three hours he talked—about himself and about the Yankees.

"There was only one Casey Stengel," Houk began. "I

am Ralph Houk. I have taken the job of managing the Yankees and I will be complete boss on the field. I did not take the job to let anyone tell me how to operate the ball club, and I don't think anyone will try. Whatever happens, I will be responsible."

After his opening statement, he was bombarded with questions. One question went this way: "What about Mickey Mantle? How important is he to the club?"

Ralph Houk, a major with the Rangers in World War II, fixed the questioner with a steady look.

"As Mantle goes," Houk said, "so go the Yankees."

A couple of months later, Ralph Houk confirmed this judgment. He announced to the press that he expected Mickey Mantle to be the leader of the club. "We talked this thing out a little," Houk said. "I told Mickey how much I would like to have him take charge of this club. I told him he meant a great deal to us.

"You need a leader, and Mantle always had so much going for him. He's one ballplayer all the players like. They look up to him and I don't think he ever realized how much they do look up to him. Now the way I figure it, if these players like him now, just think how much they'll like him if he goes out and shows them the way."

So what did Mantle do? He reported to spring training camp two days ahead of schedule, which was something for him. And he said he sure would like to be the team's inspirational leader. He put himself 100 percent behind the new manager. He said he was looking forward to his best year.

He really felt that way. It had been a good winter for Mickey. He had been less involved in business than ever before. He had disposed of his bowling alley. His only big outside interest now was a motel in Joplin, Missouri, and a boat company in Henderson, Texas. "But I'm letting other people worry about them," Mickey said. "I have no other interest now but baseball."

He had more time with his family—now three boys—and more time for hunting and golf, which had become his favorite hobbies.

For the first time in three years, Mickey signed a contract without visible fuss. He got $75,000, a $10,000 raise over the year before, his best contract as a Yankee. He felt that the new Yankee team—general manager Roy Hamey and manager Ralph Houk—appreciated him more than the old team. At the signing, Mickey was asked about Ralph Houk.

"A manager can't hit and run for you," Mickey said. "He can only command respect. If he has the team's respect, he can do all right."

Not that the Yankees didn't always try to win for Casey Stengel. Of course, they did. And Mantle always respected Stengel as a manager. "The things he said to me and about me I always figured were for my own good," Mickey once said.

But with Ralph Houk, it was more than respect. Mickey and Houk come from the same part of the country (Ralph is a Kansan), they played together on the Yankees; they had a much closer personal relationship than Stengel and Mantle.

Mickey was one of the first to call Ralph and congratulate him on getting the job. It was then that Houk mentioned the possibilities of Mickey becoming the team leader. Ralph told Mickey, "To be a leader, you run out every pop fly and cheap ground ball, then maybe the rest of the players will run them out, too." And Ralph added, "You've got to cut down on your swing."

In 1960 Mickey had struck out 125 times. There were other problems, too.

In 1960 Mickey had hit .349 right-handed, only .247 left-handed. "I don't know what's happened to me," Mickey said, "but I don't feel right batting left-handed. I just can't swing. The ball seems to jump at me when I'm up left-handed, and I can't seem to pull the trigger. During the last month of the season, I hit nine homers—five of them righty. But even the homers I got left-handed didn't feel good. I didn't think I hit them flush."

As far as giving up switch-hitting, Mickey had softened his position, a little. He said, "If I were playing regularly in Fenway Park or Griffith Stadium, where the righty homer is easy and the lefty homer very hard, I'd consider changing, and becoming strictly a right-handed hitter. But in Yankee Stadium, which favors the lefty, it would be silly."

What, a reporter wanted to know, were Mickey's goals in 1961?

Mickey said, "I'll settle for a .300 batting average, 100 runs batted in and 40 homers."

It was a firm enough goal for a Mickey Mantle. And at Florida in the spring of 1961, Mickey looked like he was going all out to achieve those goals.

It was the best spring of Mickey's major league career. The "new" Mickey Mantle look seemed apparent to everyone who saw Mickey at St. Petersburg. He was a veteran now with ten years behind him, a wife, three children, a mature twenty-nine years old. The blond crew-cut Mantle, maybe ten pounds heavier than he was in

1951 when he first reported to the Yankees, had had ten productive years. He had averaged 140 games, 500 times at bat, 111 runs scored, 154 hits, 22 doubles, 6 triples, 34 home runs and 94 runs batted in each season. His lifetime batting average of .307 was as good as any active player in the league.

Now he was relaxed, confident, approachable. In the field, he was hitting the ball solidly from both sides of the plate. He was fielding flawlessly. His aches and pains were minor ones. And, slowly, he began to assume the leadership that had been handed to him.

"He's grown up," Ralph Houk said, watching Mickey that spring. "He's a man now. Mature. I think his mind's at ease and it shows in the way he plays. He's happy about the money he's getting and that makes a difference, too. He should have a big year."

It started out that way, for sure. Mickey began banging right from opening day. The Yankees won ten of their first sixteen games. And *seven* of them were decided by the big bat of Mickey Charles Mantle. He blasted eight home runs in those games—six of them decisive blows that won ball games. He was leading the league in home runs and runs batted in, he was fielding spectacularly, and he was running the bases as only Mickey Mantle, when sound, can.

Some for instances.

On April 17 the Yankees won 3–0. Mickey hit a two-run homer in the first inning, knocked in the other run in the third with a single, went 3 for 4 and stole a base.

On April 21 Mickey hit a 380-foot homer to give Whitey Ford a 4–2 victory.

On April 26 the Yankees faced the Detroit Tigers, who

had won ten games in a row. The Yankees scored five runs to open it, then got another in the top of the second to make it 6–0. But the Tigers stormed back in the bottom of the second with four runs on a homer by Rocky Colavito, two singles, a double and a wild throw by Elston Howard. The Yankees picked up two more in the next three innings, but in the bottom of the seventh the Tigers erupted for five more runs to go ahead, 11–8.

In the top of the eighth, Bobby Richardson singled, and scored on a double by Kubek. With relief pitcher Jim Donohue on the mound, Mantle came up left-handed. He hit a long home run to tie the score.

The game went into the tenth inning, and now lefty Hank Aguirre was on the mound. Hector Lopez singled and Mickey came up to the plate batting right-handed. He ripped the home run that gave the Yankees the ball game, 13–11.

On May 2, Mickey did it again. This time he hit a low, outside fast ball thrown by Camilo Pascual. He hit it with the bases loaded in the tenth inning to give the Yankees a 6–4 victory over the Minnesota Twins. It was the sixth grand slam of Mickey's career.

Present at that game in Minneapolis, the first game the Yankees had played in the new major league baseball city, was general manager Roy Hamey. He was impressed by Mickey's blast. "You can't put a price on that kind of talent," Hamey raved.

"Would you take a million dollars for him?" Hamey was asked.

"He's not for sale and everybody knows it," Roy said. "But a million dollars wouldn't take care of the first payment. You can't measure the value of this kind of a ball-

player to us. You certainly can't measure what he's been
to us this year."

After the game, Mickey told how he had heeded Houk's
advice. He had cut down on his swing. "I got a lot of wrist
action in the swing," he said. A teammate, Tony Kubek,
shook his head.

"Mickey just flicked his bat at that pitch and it went 430
feet. That's the secret, but only if you've got the kind of
coordination and talent Mickey's got."

By May 4, Mickey was batting .325 with 9 home runs
and 23 runs batted in.

But it was even more than that. In one early May game
against Washington, Mickey stole second base twice with
two outs. One of the steals led directly to a Yankee run.
The Yankees won, 4–3.

"As Mantle goes, so go the Yankees." It was so true,
especially in the early going that season of 1961, before
Roger Maris started exploding home runs. When Mickey
went into a slight seven-game batting slump in May, the
Yankees lost five of those games. Then when he bounced
back, the Yankees bounced back.

The bouncing back came on Sunday, May 14, when the
Yankees played another crucial doubleheader with the
Tigers. If Detroit won the two games, they would move
six and a half games out in front of the Yankees. If the
Yankees won two, the lead would be cut to two and a
half games.

Going into the game, the slump-shackled Mantle was
down to .279. He came out of that doubleheader with a
batting average of .309.

In the first game, won by the Yankees 5–4 in 11 innings,
Mickey had two singles and a double, and he scored the

winning run in the 11th inning after he had opened with a single.

Mickey's leg was bothering him and Houk was inclined to rest Mantle in the second game, but Mickey insisted on playing. So he played and got two hits and scored three runs and stole a base. The Yankees won, 8–6. All in all that happy afternoon, Mickey had five for eight—two walks, a stolen base, five runs scored; and he was involved in five of the six Yankee scoring innings. That double-header illustrated the importance of Mickey Mantle to the ball club. He didn't hit a home run all afternoon, yet without him in the lineup it is questionable whether the Yankees would have even taken one of the games.

As the season progressed, the Yankees, Indians and Tigers in a roaring three-way fight for first place, Mickey continued to have trouble with his legs. But, as always, he tried to ignore the pain. One May 27 he had to pull out of a doubleheader with the White Sox because of an ailing right leg. But on May 29 against the Red Sox in Boston, his legs heavily bandaged, Mickey was back in the starting lineup. He hit a home run against Ike Delock, the one Yankee run as the Red Sox won, 11–1.

On Memorial Day, the Yankees again played at Boston. In the first inning, two men on base, Mickey came to bat left-handed against Gene Conley. His right wrist was bandaged—he had sprained it earlier in the season. His leg was sore. The count went to three balls and one strike. On the next pitch, Mickey swung and missed. He winced visibly and stepped away from the plate. You could see the pain etched on his face. He took a couple of practice swings out of the box to test himself. Then he stepped back in.

He fouled off a pitch and then, on Conley's next delivery, Mickey boomed one into the right-field bleachers, his 12th home run of the year.

He hit one more that day as the Yankees, altogether, smashed seven home runs against the Red Sox, winning 12–3.

On May 31, Mickey hit another homer—four home runs in three days.

On June 13 the Yankees met the Indians in the first crucial series of the year. The Indians were in first place by a game. They were in first place by two games after the opener, won by Cleveland 7–2. But the Yankees won the second game. So it came down to the clutch third game.

The Indians scored first when Woodie Held singled and Bubba Phillips doubled. It was 1–0 going into the top of the seventh. Mickey came up and did just what the Yankee fans were imploring him to do. He hit a long home run to tie the score. The Yankees went on to win it in 11 innings.

On July 2, at Yankee Stadium, Mickey hit a home run against the Senators. It was his 1000th major league run batted in.

The month of July the Yankees ripped through the league winning 20 games and losing only nine. The big heroes were Mantle and Maris, who were blasting home runs at a phenomenal rate. Mickey was never happier.

At Washington on July 18, Mickey participated in a home run contest. Elston Howard couldn't hit one out of the park in five tries. Roger Maris made it once. Mickey Mantle came up right-handed. Johnny Blanchard, normally a catcher, or outfielder, pitched to Mickey. Mickey hit two home runs on the first four tries. On the last pitch he unloaded one that ricocheted in the superstructure of a light tower and bounced out of the park. Mickey came back to the dugout with a big grin on his face.

The grin lasted for the game itself. His first time up, Mickey put the Yankees ahead with a two-run homer over the 31-foot wall in right field. His last time up in the eighth, he put the Yankees ahead 4–3 with another home run, a shot which carried over the billboard which sits on top of the 31-foot fence. That put him in a tie with Roger Maris for the home run lead, 35 apiece.

After the game, Mickey was asked how it felt to catch up to Maris. "As long as I'm hitting," he said, "I don't care if he hits 80. I'll hit 81."

"You really seem to be enjoying yourself," a reporter said.

"This is a good, good game, when you're going good. But when you're not . . ." Mickey let his words trail off.

Both Maris, who also had 35 homers, and Mantle were 17 games ahead of Babe Ruth's 1927 pace, the year Ruth hit 60 home runs. But between Maris and Mantle, there was no doubt in Ralph Houk's mind who was the leader of the ball club. Houk said, "Mickey's been playing so great he has inspired all of us. Every man on this team looks up to Mickey because of the way he has been handling himself out on the ball field. And I'm not only talking about his home runs. Look at the statistics sheet. He's got more walks than anybody. He's scored more runs than anybody. He's got more total bases than anybody. He's stolen seven bases and nobody's thrown him out yet. He's hit into only two double plays. He's hustling. He's fielding."

On July 21, the Yankees went into first place. They beat the Red Sox, 11–7. Roger Maris hit his 36th home run. Mickey Mantle hit his 37th.

On August 6, Mickey had his biggest day of the year.

The Yankees were playing a doubleheader with the Minnesota Twins. The first game went 15 innings before the Yankees pulled it out, 7–6. Mickey went 4 for 6—two home runs, a single, a double, three runs batted in, two walks and a stolen base.

The Yankees won the second game, 3–2. Mickey hit another one. Three home runs for the day—his 41st, 42nd, 43rd of the season. That put him two up on teammate Maris and sixteen days ahead of Babe Ruth's 1927 mark.

He was happy. He was playing superb ball and even his mistakes were going for him. In a game against the Twins in the tenth inning, two outs, Mickey walked. Yogi Berra hit a single into right field. Mickey paused, then lit off for second. Bob Allison threw the ball into second but nobody was there. Mantle took off for third.

Ted Lepcio, the third baseman, fielded the ball in short left. Bob Pleis, the pitcher, covered third and Mickey was hung up. Lepcio ran in with the ball and faked a throw. Mickey stopped and faked back to second. Then he faked towards third. Suddenly, after a few more fakes between Lepcio and Mantle, Mickey made a belly slide into third. Lepcio threw the ball to the wrong side of the bag and Mickey was safe. John Blanchard came up and hit a home run that won the game.

Afterward, they asked Mickey what had happened.

He laughed. "I was gonna stop at second," he said, "until I saw the ball go by the shortstop. That's when I put my head to work. But when I saw the pitcher at third I said to myself, 'I'll fake back to second and fake to third and he'll throw the ball bad and I'll slide in head first,' and that's the way it was." The reporters roared in appreciation.

The betting by August 6 was on Mickey Mantle, not

Roger Maris, to beat out the Babe. But a combination of circumstances, including illnesses, injuries and too careful pitching, slowed Mickey up.

Of his next four home runs, Mickey said three of them were hit off bad pitches. His 47th home run, hit in Minneapolis, came on a low change-up thrown by left-hander Jim Kaat on a 2–2 count. "That pitch would have bounced in front of the plate if I hadn't reached out and hit it," Mickey said. The ball landed about a dozen rows up in the left-field bleachers.

In one game against the Indians, Mickey Mantle was actually walked intentionally in the *first* inning, with John Blanchard, a hot batter, coming up.

The Yankees' most vital series of the year began on September 1 against the Tigers. Detroit wheeled into Yankee Stadium only a game and a half behind the Yankees. The American League standings read like this:

1. New York   87–45
2. Detroit   86–47

If Detroit could win three straight, the Tigers would leave town in first place by a game and a half. Even if they could take two of three, it would still be pretty good, a mere half-game behind.

The Yankee players knew the stakes. That's all they talked about in the days preceding the game. Driving from the apartment they shared in Queens, a borough of New York City, Roger Maris, Mickey Mantle and Bob Cerv talked about the series.

"What do you think we need?" Cerv asked.

"If we can just take two of them," Mickey said, "they're going to have a rough time catching us."

Roger said, "If we can take the first two, I'll bet we sweep the series."

The Yankees went to work slowly. Mickey Mantle was especially slow. In the opener against left-hander Don Mossi, Mickey struck out three times, looking futile against Mossi. After one of those strikeouts, a batting helmet kicked out of the dugout and rolled toward the backstop. It didn't take much imagination to figure out who had done the kicking. But the Yankees rallied to win the game, 1–0.

In the second game the Tigers jumped out in front 2–0 in the first inning on a Rocky Colavito home run. But the Yankees clawed back.

In the second inning, Mickey walked and Bill Skowron doubled him home. In the fourth Mickey dragged a sacrifice bunt down the first-base line to score Maris.

In the sixth inning, Mickey chopped a grounder to second and pulled a muscle in his left forearm with the swing. He barely ran out the ball because of the pain, but the fans immediately started booing him, thinking he was not hustling.

Ralph Houk decided to keep Mickey in the game. "He was in pain," Houk said later, "but I needed him in center field. I didn't want to go making lineup changes at a time like that. We were only winning three to two."

Besides, Mickey begged to stay in the game. "I can still run and catch the ball," he told Houk. "And when I come up to bat, I'll bunt."

So Mickey came up in the ninth, bases empty, and bunted. And he beat it out. The Yankees won, 7–2.

When Mickey woke up on Sunday morning, game No. 3 scheduled against the Tigers, he found he could barely raise the arm. He went out to the park and told Houk.

"If you can play," Ralph said, "let me know."

Mickey took some whirlpool treatments, then felt his

arm loosen up a bit and he told his manager, "I can play."

And play he did. Before the game he conferred with roommate Bob Cerv about using one of Cerv's bats. Normally, Mickey uses a 33- or 34-ounce bat, but with his arm hurt, he couldn't bear the pain missing a swing. So he asked Cerv for one of his 36-ounce bats, the heaviest on the club. "That way I figured I would be forced to swing easier because I simply couldn't get the ball around as fast."

In the bottom of the first, tough Jim Bunning in there against the Yankees, Maris singled. Mickey came up left-handed. The count went to 3–2. Then Bunning came in with a low fast ball. Mickey swung easily, lashing the heavy bat almost one-handed, like a tennis player executing a backhand stroke. The ball literally leaped into the right-field stands on a hot low line for his 49th home run of the season.

But the Tigers fought back and in the bottom of the ninth they led, 5–4. Mickey was the first batter. "He was in agony out there," Houk recalled, "but I figured he had gone this far, he just might bust one." The pitcher was Gerry Staley, with that tricky sinker ball. Staley got it over too high. Again, Mickey swung one-handed. This time the ball took a long, slow, majestic arch deep into the right center-field bleachers for the tying run. The Yankees went on to win the game, 8–5. The rout was on. The Yankees won thirteen straight games and turned the American League pennant race upside down again.

The last month of the baseball season—while Roger Maris was electrifying the baseball world with his home run feats, hitting No. 61 on the last day of the season—was a nightmare month for Mickey. He developed a bad cold, which became a low-grade virus infection. Then he contracted an abscess on his thigh. He was out of the lineup starting September 18, though he had staggered around with the cold at least a week before that date. On September 25 he returned to play against the Red Sox, hitting his 54th home run of the season to help Whitey Ford win his 25th game.

That was his last home run, and his last appearance of the season. Immediately after the game he suffered a relapse and was sent to the hospital where he underwent surgery for the abscess.

But it had been another super year for Mantle. He had batted .317, his highest average in four years. He led the league in runs scored with 132. He walked oftener (126 times) and was on base more than anyone else. He drove in 128 runs. He led the league in slugging percentage, .687, and the club in stolen bases, 12. Of his 54 home runs, 2 won games in the last inning, 3 tied up games, 13 ultimately proved to be the winning run. He was an inspirational ballplayer, a leader.

It was his best year since 1956, and there were reasons.

One was the challenge laid down by Roger Maris. Maris proved an inspiration to Mickey. Mickey had been number one man on the club and then Roger came along; Mickey rose to the challenge.

There was some talk during the season about how jealous Mickey was of Roger, and vice versa. This was not true. They lived together in New York, they respected each other, they kidded each other all the time.

Mickey told Roger once that if he came up to try for

number 60, Mickey would ask the umpire to look at his bat and throw it out of the game. Roger retaliated by telling Mantle, "If you hit sixty, and I'm on base, I'll run the wrong way, so I'll be automatically out."

Mickey told Bob Cerv, who lived with them too, when Roger hit number 60, "He deserves all the credit in the world. I'm very happy for him."

The three shared a $250-a-month apartment in perfect harmony. Often, Roger would drive Mickey's 1961 white Oldsmobile convertible during the 25-minute trip from their Jamaica, Long Island, apartment to Yankee Stadium.

"It would be foolish of me to say that Roger and Mickey weren't conscious of each other," said Cerv. "They were. They both admitted many times that while they wished the other fellow luck, this was competition for the greatest honor in baseball and Mickey was rooting for Mickey and Roger was rooting for Roger. But that had nothing to do with the respect they had for one another.

"If there was any professional jealousy between them," Cerv said, "they did a pretty good job of hiding it, I can tell you that."

The great Mantle-Maris duel of 1961 did have one pofound effect on Mickey—that was his relationship with his public. As Maris began to challenge Babe Ruth's record, Mickey Mantle began more and more to get the sympathy of the fans. They wanted Mickey to break Babe Ruth's record. When Mickey hit his 52nd home run of the season against the Indians on September 2, the 42,000 fans in the stadium stood and applauded while he rounded the bases.

"Those fans!" Mickey marveled. "They've changed. I never heard so much cheering in all my years with the club. For the first time, I felt like I was playing before a home crowd, before *our* fans. Before, it was like we were playing on the road. They've never been so good to me. It seems too nice."

Phil Rizzuto, the Yankee broadcaster, later said, "I don't think the fans were applauding Mickey that day simply because he was the underdog to Roger Maris. I think they were applauding him, as they did that last month of the season, because they had begun to realize the kind of courage Mickey Mantle possesses. He played games where you or I or the normal guy would probably not have been able to creep out of bed. But Mantle is not the normal type of guy."

Mickey gave an example of that courage in the World Series against Cincinnati.

Mickey sat out the first two games. He played in pain in the third game, and got no hits. In the fourth inning of the fourth game, Maris walked off Jim O'Toole. Mickey Mantle came up. He drove a ball to left field. It would have been an easy double for Mickey if he were feeling normal, but he barely made it to first base. He limped off the field, blood running from the abscess in his thigh and soaking through his uniform. People who saw his wound said it was so deep you could see the thigh muscles. Mickey played no more in that Series.

One writer said, "It was a sad, uncomfortable sight to see him dragging his big body to first base. He looked like some horribly wounded animal trying with all its heart to escape a hunter's bullet."

The Yankees won the Series in five games.

It was Roger Maris who destroyed Babe Ruth's sacrosanct home run record. And it was Roger Maris who, for the second straight year, won the American League Most

Valuable Player award. This time he beat out Mantle by four votes, even though the two New York voters, John Drebinger of *The New York Times,* and Dan Daniel of the New York *World Telegram and Sun,* had cast their ballots for Mantle.

"Mickey was the most valuable player on the team beyond any question," said a Yankee official. "The writers gave the MVP to Maris, but our players would have given it to Mantle. Maris would have, too."

The leader had led.

CHAPTER FIFTEEN

PAIN AND TRIUMPH

The thud was literally heard around the baseball world.

It happened on the night of May 18, 1962, the Yankees playing the Minnesota Twins at Yankee Stadium.

The Yankees were tied for first place with the Indians. Each team had an 18–11 record. Breathing hard behind them were the Twins, with a 19–13 record. And Mickey Mantle was off to one of his best starts. He was batting .315 with 7 home runs and 18 runs batted in.

The game came down to the last half of the ninth inning and the surprising Twins held a 4–3 lead over the Yankees. Don Lee was the pitcher, rookie Tom Tresh was on second base, there were two out, and Mickey Mantle was coming up. Minnesota manager Sam Mele decided a fresh pitcher ought to face Mantle. He came out to the mound, patted Lee and waved to his bullpen. Left-hander Dick Stigman came in.

Mele waited on the mound for Stigman. "Don't give him anything good to hit," the manager said. "Give him low curve balls. I don't care if you walk him." Stigman nodded.

But on the first pitch, Stigman made a mistake. He threw a curve ball that came in high and Mantle, batting right-handed, swung. Mickey was just a little on top of the ball but still it was a smasher, a low line drive that sped past the third baseman before he could blink his eyes. But then the ball hit the dirt and fast-moving short-stop Zoiolo Versalles, who had gotten a good jump, stuck his glove out. The ball hit it, then bounced out.

Mantle saw all this and thought to himself, "If I can get there fast, I can beat his throw." Straining all the muscles in his heavily muscled body, Mickey tried for that extra burst of speed. Suddenly, 25 feet from first base, he fell.

To the spectators, Mantle dropped like he was shot. To Mickey Mantle, it felt like somebody had taken a knife and stuck it in his right leg. One moment the leg was up in the air, the next moment—at the knife thrust—the leg had collapsed, like air rushing out of a balloon.

As he went down, Mickey also felt a stabbing pain in his left knee. He lay face down in the damp ground, his fingernails clutching at the grass. He lashed at himself in frustration. "You hurt yourself again. You hurt yourself again."

Wally Moses, the first-base coach, had been watching

Versalles. "Then," he remembered, "I looked for Mantle; he was already down."

The crowd rose to its feet sorrowfully, standing hushed and silent. The game was over but nobody moved. On television and on radio, wherever the game was heard, nobody moved. At the stadium and in the homes, the plea was, "Come on, Mickey, get up." Behind the plea was the dark thought that Mickey might be hurt so badly, his career would be endangered.

Mickey did not get up. For five minutes he lay on the base paths while his anxious teammates, the trainer, the manager, umpires, groped around him. Bob Cerv moaned, "He's hurt. He's hurt real bad."

They brought out the stretcher but Mickey refused it. He put his arms around old Wally Moses and around young Tom Tresh, and he leaned heavily on them as they slowly lifted him off the ground and carried him to the Yankee clubhouse.

Inside the locker room, Mickey took his shower on crutches. He came back and dressed slowly, his face gray and pain-flecked. Then, fully dressed, he managed a tired grin. "See you all," he said. He was driven to the hospital by Dan Topping, co-owner of the Yankees, and Bob Fishel, the club's publicity director.

Later a report was issued on Mantle's condition. There was a tear of the adductor muscle of the right upper thigh. It was called "reasonably severe." X-rays were also taken of the right groin area and left knee. No breaks. The left knee seemed only bruised.

Ralph Houk went home but didn't go to bed until 4 in the morning after hearing about Mantle's condition. And even then Ralph had trouble sleeping. "When it happened," he remembered, "I thought he was hurt even worse than he was. I thought maybe he'd broken his leg. That was a real sick feeling. That was the only game I've ever been in I didn't think about losing."

That night, the Yankees fell into third place.

It had been a wonderful winter for the "new" Mickey Mantle. It seemed as though everyone recognized the change that had come over the thirty-year-old super hero. The pressure of the terrific 1961 home run duel between Maris and Mantle, the fact that Roger Maris had beaten Babe Ruth while Mickey Mantle nursed injuries, seemed to have completed the cycle of sympathy and understanding for Mickey that had begun late in 1960 when he was pulled out of a ball game for "loafing." Now, Mickey Mantle was being accepted for what he was—and that was the rightful heir to Ruth, Gehrig and DiMaggio. He knew it, too, and this helped change his own character.

"I care much more about other people's feelings now," is how Mickey put it. "I used to think, what the heck, and not waste any time with them. Now I realize they have feelings, too."

As the world turned more pleasant towards Mantle, he turned more pleasant towards the world.

And so it was a delightful winter. The pressure was all on Roger Maris, who had hit the 61 home runs, and Mickey was able to relax more than he ever had. He hunted, he played golf, he saw more of his family—his wife Merlyn, his four children, Mickey, Jr., who was eight; David, then six; Bill, four; and Dan, two.

He was also making a lot of money in extracurricular appearances. Frank Scott, Mickey's enterprising agent, closed a deal for Mickey and Maris to endorse a kind of habadashery called "Mantle-Maris Wear." For use of their names, M & M received advances of $25,000 each. Each also would receive 1 percent of the gross—which some business experts felt could bring an annual income of $125,000 to both Mantle and Maris.

Then Scott signed Mickey and Roger for a movie, *Safe at Home,* in which they would co-star. Mickey came into New York for the signing. With newspapermen around he looked at himself in the mirror and said, "You handsome dog, you."

Another time, leaving his hotel, Mickey got into his car, then noticed a pretty woman step off the curb and raise her arm in a signal for a taxi. "Darn," Mickey said, "I keep telling her not to wave at me right in the street like that."

The next time he came into New York, it was to sign his contract for an estimated $82,000, the highest salary of his career. At the signing, attended by manager Ralph Houk, Mickey was asked if he would repeat his 1961 promise—that he would help the inexperienced Houk win a pennant.

"This is Ralph's second year." Mickey grinned. "He's on his own now."

Afterward, for the benefit of photographers, Mickey posed signing a blank contract. In the space reserved for salary figures he inserted his own special conditions: "All expenses paid. No curfew."

Then late in January, Mickey came in for the annual New York baseball writers banquet. On the dais were such people as Bob Feller and Jackie Robinson, the two newest members of the Hall of Fame; and Roger Maris,

Casey Stengel, Ralph Houk and Mickey Mantle. Mickey was the hit of the night.

He was called on to speak after Stengel, who had rambled on in his own unique fashion, full of double-talk and witty asides. How could you top Stengel? Mantle managed.

"I had a terrific speech prepared," Mickey said, "but I had some trouble. I was walking on the street and I bumped into a fellow I recognized. It was Casey. He told me he was supposed to speak here tonight, but he didn't know what to say. I pitied him because he was always good to me, and so I gave him my speech."

The audience roared and Mickey grinned. "And you know something?" he went on. "That son of a gun not only used my speech, he went and memorized it."

Mickey brought down the house. Some 1,400 people were surprised by Mickey's poise, including his manager Ralph Houk. "You know," Ralph said. "I sat there listening to him and I was very pleased, but I was also amazed. You know, it was funny. He wound up like a lot of us, not knowing how to get off."

"I understand he's been that way all winter," Bob Fishel said. "They tell me he was great in Dallas."

How had this all happened? Ralph Houk had one answer, and it made a lot of sense. Houk said, "I think he's learned to appreciate that it isn't just that he's given a lot to baseball, but that baseball has given a lot to him."

At Fort Lauderdale, Florida, the Yankees' new spring base, Mantle was loose and confident. He felt strong physically, and he was hitting the ball on the nose. He expected to have a good year.

It started out that way. On May 5, Mickey hit a home

run against the Senators. On May 6, in a doubleheader, he had a single and a home run, two runs batted in in the first game; two home runs and three RBI's in the second game—three homers and five RBI's for the day.

But Mickey had a premonition. The Sunday before his injury against the Twins, Mickey played a doubleheader in Cleveland, then got into a team bus for a three-hour ride to Pittsburgh. There was an exhibition game with the Pirates that night and then a plane trip to Boston after the game. When the chartered DC-7 got to Boston, it couldn't land because of fog. It turned around and at 5 A.M., landed at Idlewild in New York. The team went to a motel and at 10 o'clock was in the air again. They played two night games and a day game in Boston, then came home to play a night game against the Twins.

"I never got rested," Mantle told New York *Post* writer Leonard Shecter. "I felt my groin getting tighter and tighter. I could feel it getting sore. Every time I pull a muscle I can feel it getting sore."

The premonition came true on the night of May 18. And once more, Mickey was lost to the Yankees.

Let us take one more look at Mantle's injuries since becoming a Yankee. If you are to appreciate Mantle completely, you must understand the handicaps under which he plays:

1951. Damaged knee in the World Series. Surgery necessary.

1953. Operation for removal of knee cartilage and torn ligament.

1954. Cyst cut from knee.

1955. Pulled thigh.

1956. Sprained ligaments and tonsillectomy.

1957. Shoulder injury, shin splints and sprained
      ligament.
1958. Bruised forearm.
1959. Fractured finger.
1961. Hip abscess.
1962. Torn adductor muscle, right leg, bruised left
      knee, groin.

Add to this list all the unreported injuries over the years, all the games Mantle played while he was in pain. Add them all together and you will see what Mantle has accomplished in his baseball lifetime.

Mickey was cheered in the hospital by baskets of fruit, stacks of mail from fans, and a bouquet of eight wilted daisies from his teammates—sent by ringleader Whitey Ford. The daisies were fair indications of the state of the team without Mickey.

His hospital stay was also made bearable by visits from teammates and friends. Ralph Houk came in and needled Mickey.

"Too bad you're hurt," he said. "But at least you'll have a chance to look at the kids."

Mickey looked horror-stricken. "I'm ready to come out of the hospital," he said.

But he stayed in five days and then went back to his family in Dallas. There he took daily therapy on his legs from Wayne Rudy, a trainer for the Dallas Texans football team.

Meanwhile, the Yankees put up a brave front. "We'll miss him," Houk said, "but we'll just have to make do with what we've got."

General manager Roy Hamey was asked what pace the Yankees would have to maintain without Mantle, to keep

alive in the pennant race. Hamey said, "If we can play
.500 ball until he gets back, then we'll be in pretty good
shape."

Hamey turned out to be a prophet. Mickey missed five
weeks of the season, 28 games. The Yankees lost 14 of
them.

Two weeks after his injury, Mickey got a call from
Hamey.

"We want you to rejoin the team," Hamey said. "The
boys will feel better if you're around."

"I'll feel better too," Mickey said.

He met the Yankees in Los Angeles. Bobby Richardson
was the first player to spot Mickey. "I just walked up to
him and shook his hand," Bobby said. "It's hard to explain, but just seeing him gave me a lift."

The Yankees won two out of three at Los Angeles to put
themselves back into a tie for first place. Mickey laughed.
"I got you into first place. Now you're on your own."

It was nice to have him around, but it would have been
even nicer if he could play. But the knee healed slowly.
One evening, before a night game, Ralph Houk jokingly
suggested that Mickey get in the game and run stiff-legged.
Houk showed him how, running down the length of the
room like a peg-legged pirate.

Mickey took batting practice with the team, with the
subs. When he missed the ball, his knees quivered like an
antenna in high wind. But when he connected, the
ball traveled with the customary Mantle vigor. One day
Mickey drove several balls into the stands and Ralph
Houk, watching, made believe he was changing his lineup
to get Mickey in. Mickey answered by limping extrava-
gantly as he left the batting cage.

He did get a little exasperated by reporters constantly asking him when he felt he would be ready to play. Once he got a piece of paper and taped it to his chest. The printed message read: "Slight improvement. Be back in two weeks." But it didn't work. People still asked him when he would be ready.

Then on June 16, he was ready.

The Yankees were playing the league-leading Cleveland Indians at Cleveland. The Indians jumped off to a six-run lead in the first two innings. Going into the top of the eighth, Cleveland led, 7–6. There was one out, two men on base, when Mickey was called over to the bat rack by Ralph Houk.

"Go on up and hit for Bridges," Houk said. "But if you hit it on the ground, don't bother to run. Give 'em the double play."

Mickey didn't hit it on the ground. He hit it in the air, high and mighty, into the stands, three runs scoring on the blast to give the Yankees a 9–7 lead. The partisan Indian fans rose as one and cheered the enemy Mantle as he limped around the bases. Mickey was mobbed as he stepped into the dugout.

As it turned out, the Yankees lost the game finally, 10–9, but it was one of the most redeeming losses they would ever suffer. They were jubilant in the dressing room. Mickey was especially happy.

"It meant a lot to me," he said simply. "It meant a lot to the team."

Mickey pinch-hit twice more, striking out once, grounding out the second time. Then, at Baltimore's Memorial Stadium on June 20, Ralph Houk held a press conference.

"Mickey will definitely start Friday night at Detroit,"

Houk said. "He will play right field. Roger Maris will move to center."

Writers pounced around Mickey and he answered questions patiently. "I'd be a liar if I told you my knee was 100 percent. But the only way I can tell how bad I really am is to try it by starting a game. I've been sitting around here doing nothing for five weeks. The knee is getting better, but it's a slow process. I want to find out how bad this thing really is."

Mickey played against Detroit on June 22, went 1 for 3, scored two runs. A teammate, Elston Howard, described the Yankees' feelings at Mickey's return. "It was one of the greatest things that happened to the club," Howard said. "You could feel the whole club pick up."

Mickey played the entire Detroit series, getting one home run. Each game he played, each game his leg felt better. And the Yankees started to move again.

At the All-Star game break, Mickey's batting average was at .333. He had hit .368 since returning to the lineup. He had 17 home runs in all, five in the Yankees' last eight games. And the Yankees as a team had won 13 and lost 6. Mickey had walked 54 times in 51 games and his on-base average was an amazing .505. Ralph Houk was elated.

The manager said, "The reason Mickey's looking so good at the plate is that he's been taking those base on balls. The way it used to be, Mickey would get tired of seeing so many balls and few strikes. Before he realized what he was doing, he'd be going after balls he should have been taking. Now, though, he's patient. You won't find him swinging at bad balls any more. As a result, he's getting better pitches to hit."

Mickey felt the same way. "When I look back," he told

The telephoto lens catches "the star of the stadium" at the plate as he studies the motions of the pitcher.

sportswriter Til Ferdenzi, "I can see a lot of times when I'd let all those walks I was getting bother me. I'd get mad and swing away. That way I was doing just what the pitchers hoped I'd do. I was going after their pitch, not mine. Usually, I'd be swinging at bad balls and popping up or not hitting them at all."

His bombing continued. From June 22, Mantle's reappearance in the starting lineup, to July 25, the Yankees' won-lost record was 22–9. In his last 17 games, Mickey was hitting .420, with 16 RBI's in that period. His average now was .342.

"There's no question that he's playing as strong a game as he has ever played," said Houk.

Mickey's teammates felt the same way. Elston Howard said, "When Mickey's going good like he has, his actions kind of spill over on everybody. Just to know he's in the lineup, ready to swing with somebody on base, gives a ball team like ours a lift it needs. He's the kind of player who has more determination and guts than you'll ever know. He's a great fighter on the field. He loves to win.

"Pretty soon you get that feeling from him," Howard went on. "He does so good himself it makes everybody want to follow his example. That's what makes him the leader. He doesn't pop off, he does things. Mickey's the number one boy, and we all know it."

Early in August, Mickey's left knee felt sore and tired and he came out of the starting lineup. He missed eight days, except for two innings, then he was back.

On August 19, against Kansas City, Mickey proved something to himself—that he could still run. In the third inning with the Yankees ahead 5–1, Mickey stole second base, then he stole third. In the fifth inning he hit a grand-slam homer off of Jerry Walker. In the sixth he hit a drive to left field and slid into second base with a double. He left the game in the sixth inning, but his contributions to the Yankees 21–7 bombardment of Kansas City were felt— a grand-slam homer, double and single, and seven runs driven in.

On September 4, Mickey pulled a muscle in his side while batting. He returned to the lineup on September 10, after missing six games. Two days earlier, the Yankees without Mantle had lost two games to Minnesota. They were now only two games behind in the loss column.

Going to the top of the fifth inning of the September 4 game against the Tigers, the Yankees were down 1–0. Then Mantle came up right-handed to face the Tiger ace, Hank Aguirre. Aguirre came in with a low curve, but Mickey was ready. He blasted the ball 450 feet into the old Tiger bullpen, behind the center-field barrier. It was Mickey Mantle's 400th major league home run and a home run he would never forget.

The Yankees went on to beat the Tigers. Mickey also contributed a rally-killing catch in the eighth inning. In the top of the ninth, after a single by Bobby Richardson, Mickey drew an intentional walk. Hector Lopez singled to center to drive in the winning run. Mantle raced to third on the hit and then scored the insurance run on a ground out. The Yankees won 3–1.

In the dressing room it was as if the Yankees had clinched the pennant. Mickey was besieged by friends congratulating him on hitting the 400th homer. That put Mickey in seventh place among the all-time home run hitters. Ahead of him were Babe Ruth (714), Jimmy Foxx (534), Ted Williams (521), Mel Ott (511), Lou Gehrig

(493) and Stan Musial (460). After the game, Mickey was asked if he thought he might someday overtake Musial.

"How old is Stan?" he asked.

"Oh, forty-one or forty-two," someone said.

"Tell you one thing," said the thirty-year-old Mantle, "I'll trade bodies with him."

The next night the Yankees beat the Tigers, 8–7. Mickey went 3 for 5. Following that, the Yankees beat Cleveland, 5–2. Mickey hit a home run and drove in three runs.

And so the Yankees were able to withstand the pressure from Minnesota and go on to win another American League pennant. And Mickey Mantle, through the worst pain he had ever endured as a ballplayer, went on to one of his most triumphant seasons.

As for the World Series, all you could say about it was that the Yankees beat the Giants in seven games. Mickey expected to do well because he was feeling well. But he managed only three hits, a .120 batting average and a bad temper.

But he could look back on the regular season with much satisfaction. It boiled down this way. Without Mantle in 47 games, the Yankees played .500 ball. With Mickey, they played .625, a pennant-winning percentage.

Missing almost a third of the season, Mickey still hit 30 home runs, in 377 at-bats and 123 games. He drove in 89 runs, scored 96 runs, was on base an amazing 50 percent of the time, was the leading slugger in the American League with a .605 percentage and ended up with a .321 batting average, only five less than league-leader Pete Runnels. He also walked 122 times and struck out only 78.

An impartial source, Bill Veeck, expressed this view of

Mantle. Said the old Yankee hater, "If Mickey Mantle doesn't get the MVP award—and get it unanimously—there should be an investigation of the writers who are doing the voting."

Well, Mickey didn't win the award unanimously. He received thirteen of the twenty first-place votes. He was the only player named on all twenty ballots. All in all, he finished with 234 votes to 152 for runner-up Bobby Richardson. It was the most one-sided vote in the American League since 1956, when a fellow name of Mickey Mantle was a unanimous choice.

When the award was announced in mid-November of 1962, Mickey was out on the golf course at Tulsa, Oklahoma. He was told that he had won the MVP for the third time. He shook his head and grinned like a small boy.

"I'm sure glad to hear it," he said. "It's what you work for all year."

Mickey said, "I thought Bobby Richardson would get it. He had a darn good year. I feel bad he couldn't have won it, too."

Someone told Mantle that if he could win a fourth MVP, he would be the first major-leaguer ever to win four Most Valuable Player awards. Mickey Mantle's eyes lit up.

"Then, I'm going to try to win another one."

At age thirty-one, there was still time. Mickey had fought through pain to triumph and there was still time to endure more pain for further triumph.

MICKEY CHARLES MANTLE

Year	Club	G	AB	R	H	2B	3B	HR	RBI	BB	SO	AVE.
1949	Independence	89	323	54	101	15	7	7	63	52	66	.313
1950	Joplin	137	519	141	199	30	12	26	136	94	90	.383
1951	New York	96	341	61	91	11	5	13	65	43	74	.267
1951	Kansas City	40	166	32	60	9	3	11	50	23	30	.361
1952	New York	142	549	94	171	37	7	23	87	75	111	.311
1953	New York	127	461	105	136	24	3	21	92	79	90	.295
1954	New York	146	543	129	163	17	12	27	102	102	107	.300
1955	New York	147	517	121	158	25	11	37	99	113	97	.306
1956	New York	150	533	132	188	22	5	52	130	112	99	.353
1957	New York	144	474	121	173	28	6	34	94	146	75	.365
1958	New York	150	519	127	158	21	1	42	97	129	120	.304
1959	New York	144	541	104	154	23	4	31	75	94	126	.285
1960	New York	153	527	119	145	17	6	40	94	111	125	.275
1961	New York	153	514	132	163	16	6	54	128	126	112	.317
1962	New York	123	377	96	121	15	1	30	89	122	78	.321
M.L. Totals		1675	5896	1341	1821	256	67	404	1152	1252	1213	.309

THE AUTHOR

Al Silverman was born in Lynn, Massachusetts. Currently editor-in-chief of *Sport* Magazine, he has been a freelance writer. His contributions have appeared in the *Saturday Evening Post, Saturday Review, Argosy, TV Guide,* and numerous other magazines. He is author of THE WORLD OF SPORT, and co-author of IMMORTAL SOUTHPAW (with Warren Spahn) and THE "MIRACLE" NEW YORK YANKEES (with Phil Rizzuto). Mr. Silverman lives in Ardsley, New York, with his wife, Rosa, and three potential ballplayers—Thomas, eight; Brian, six; and Matthew, five.

Index

223